W9-BER-092

DISCARDED

FOR REFERENCE

Do Not Take From This Room

WORLD OF ANIMALS

7

MAMMALS

RODENTS 1

Squirrels, Rats, Mice ...

PAT MORRIS, AMY-JANE BEER

GROLIER

Representative species of New World rats and mice: Central American climbing rat (1); South American climbing rat (2); pygmy mouse (3); wood rat carrying a bone (4).

Published 2003 by Grolier,
Danbury, CT 06816
A division of Scholastic Library Publishing

This edition published exclusively for the school and library market

Planned and produced by
Andromeda Oxford Limited
11–13 The Vineyard,
Abingdon, Oxon OX14 3PX

www.andromeda.co.uk

Copyright © Andromeda Oxford Limited 2003

All rights reserved. No part of this publication may be reproduced, stored in a retrieval system, or transmitted in any form or by any means electronic, mechanical, photocopying, recording, or otherwise, without the permission of the copyright holder.

Library of Congress Cataloging-in-Publication Data

Morris, Pat.
    Mammals / [Pat Morris, Amy-Jane Beer, Erica Bower].
        p. cm. -- (World of animals)
    Contents: v. 1. Small carnivores -- v. 2. Large carnivores -- v. 3. Sea mammals -- v. 4. Primates -- v. 5. Large herbivores -- v. 6. Ruminant (horned) herbivores -- v. 7. Rodents 1 -- v. 8. Rodents 2 and lagomorphs -- v. 9. Insectivores and bats -- v. 10. Marsupials.
    ISBN 0-7172-5742-8 (set : alk. paper) -- ISBN 0-7172-5743-6 (v.1 : alk. paper) -- ISBN 0-7172-5744-4 (v.2 : alk. paper) -- ISBN 0-7172-5745-2 (v.3 : alk. paper) -- ISBN 0-7172-5746-0 (v.4 : alk. paper) -- ISBN 0-7172-5747-9 (v.5 : alk. paper) -- ISBN 0-7172-5748-7 (v.6 : alk. paper) -- ISBN 0-7172-5749-5 (v.7 : alk. paper) -- ISBN 0-7172-5750-9 (v.8 : alk. paper) -- ISBN 0-7172-5751-7 (v.9 : alk. paper) -- ISBN 0-7172-5752-5 (v.10 : alk. paper)
    1. Mammals--Juvenile literature. [1. Mammals.] I. Beer, Amy-Jane. II. Bower, Erica. III. Title. IV. World of animals (Danbury, Conn.)

QL706.2 .M675 2003
599--dc21

2002073860

Project Director: Graham Bateman
Editors: Angela Davies, Penny Mathias
Art Editor and Designer: Steve McCurdy
Cartographic Editor: Tim Williams
Editorial Assistants: Marian Dreier, Rita Demetriou
Picture Manager: Claire Turner
Picture Researcher: Vickie Walters
Production: Clive Sparling
Researchers: Dr. Erica Bower, Rachael Brooks, Rachael Murton, Eleanor Thomas

Origination: Unifoto International, South Africa

Printed in China

Set ISBN 0-7172-5742-8

About This Volume

In this volume we introduce the common features of all rodents and then describe those animals that have squirrel-, beaver-, and mouselike forms and lifestyles. About a third of all mammals are rodents. There are so many species that in this set Volumes 7 and 8 have been assigned to them. Although rodents are not large, the biggest being only pig-sized, some of them are outstandingly abundant. Many are capable of breeding several times a year, with litters of 10 or more offspring produced each time. Rodents are found on all the continents. A few species of rats and mice, for example, have been accidentally transported throughout the world by humans, even to the Antarctic. Rodents inhabit a variety of environments from forests to deserts, farmland, and towns. None live in the sea, but a few are semiaquatic. Many burrow, but others live their life in trees, where a few have developed the capability of long-distance gliding. While rats and mice fill many people with horror, they are also among the most popular and commonly kept pet animals. Domesticated forms have proved enormously valuable in medical research, but many wild rodents are serious pests of crops and stored food. Some rodents also carry dangerous diseases.

Contents

Ord's kangaroo rat has powerful back legs and can leap up to 6.5 feet (2 m) in a single bound.

The mzab gundi (1) is a relatively quiet member of the gundi species. Others, such as Speke's gundi (2) and the felou gundi (3), have a wide repertoire of sounds.

How to Use This Set

World of Animals: Mammals is a 10-volume set that describes in detail mammals from all corners of the earth. Each volume brings together those animals that are most closely related and have similar lifestyles. So all the meat-eating groups (carnivores) are in Volumes 1 and 2, and all the seals, whales, and dolphins (sea mammals) are in Volume 3, and so on. To help you find volumes that interest you, look at pages 6 to 7 (Find the Animal). A brief introduction to each volume is also given on page 2 (About This Volume).

Article Styles

Articles are of three kinds. There are two types of introductory or review article: One introduces large animal groups like orders (such as whales and dolphins). Another introduces smaller groups like families (The Raccoon Family, for example). The articles review the full variety of animals to be found in different groups. The third type of article makes up most of each volume. It concentrates on describing individual animals typical of the group in great detail, such as the tiger. Each article starts with a fact-filled **data panel** to help you gather information at-a-glance. Used together, the three article styles enable you to become familiar with specific animals in the context of their evolutionary history and biological relationships.

Data panel presents basic statistics of each animal

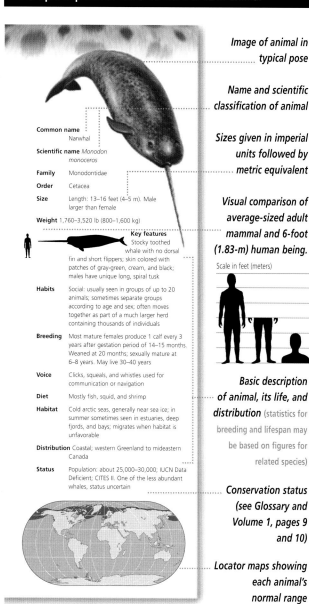

Image of animal in typical pose

Name and scientific classification of animal

Sizes given in imperial units followed by metric equivalent

Visual comparison of average-sized adult mammal and 6-foot (1.83-m) human being.

Basic description of animal, its life, and distribution (statistics for breeding and lifespan may be based on figures for related species)

Conservation status (see Glossary and Volume 1, pages 9 and 10)

Locator maps showing each animal's normal range

Article describes a particular animal

Scientific name of animal

Common name of animal

Captions to photographs provide additional information about each animal's lifestyle

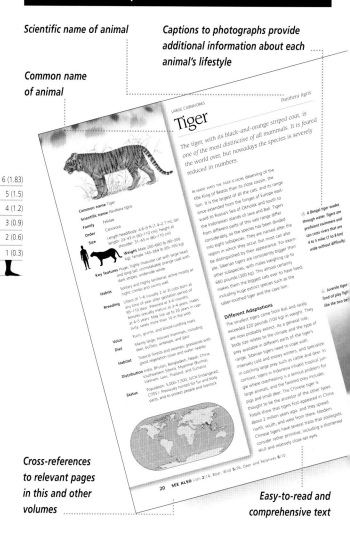

Cross-references to relevant pages in this and other volumes

Easy-to-read and comprehensive text

A number of other features help you navigate through the volumes and present you with helpful extra information. At the bottom of many pages are **cross-references** to other articles of interest. They may be to related animals, animals that live in similar places, animals with similar behavior, predators (or prey), and much more. Each volume also contains a **Set Index** to the complete *World of Animals: Mammals*. All animals mentioned in the text are indexed by common and scientific names, and many topics are also covered. A **Glossary** will also help you if there are words used in the text that you do not fully understand. Each volume ends with a list of useful **Further Reading and Websites** that help you take your research further. Finally, under the heading "List of Species" you will find expanded listings of the animals that are covered in each volume.

Introductory article describes family or closely related groups

Detailed maps clarify animal's distribution

At-a-glance boxes cover topics of special interest

Meticulous drawings illustrate a typical selection of group members

Tables summarize classification of groups and give scientific names of animals mentioned in the text

Who's Who tables summarize classification of each major group and give scientific names of animals mentioned in the text

Introductory article describes major groups of animals

Graphic full-color photographs bring text to life

Detailed diagrams illustrate text

Find the Animal

World of Animals: Mammals is the first part of a library that describes all groups of living animals. Each cluster of volumes in *World of Animals* will cover a familiar group of animals—mammals, birds, reptiles and amphibians, fish, and insects and other invertebrates. These groups also represent categories of animals recognized by scientists (see The Animal Kingdom below).

The Animal Kingdom

The living world is divided into five kingdoms, one of which (kingdom Animalia) is the main subject of the

World of Animals. Also included are those members of the kingdom Protista that were once regarded as animals, but now form part of a group that includes all single-cell organisms. Kingdom Animalia is divided into numerous major groups called Phyla, but only one of them (Chordata) contains those animals that have a backbone. Chordates, or vertebrates as they are popularly known, include all the animals familiar to us and those most studied by scientists—mammals, birds, reptiles, amphibians, and fish. In all, there are about 38,000 species of vertebrates, while the Phyla that contain animals without backbones (so-called invertebrates, such as insects, spiders, and so on) include at least 1 million species, probably many more. To find which set of volumes in the *World of Animals* is relevant to you, see the chart Main Groups of Animals (page 7).

Mammals in Particular

World of Animals: Mammals focuses on the most familiar of animals, those most easily recognized as having fur (although this may be absent in many sea mammals like whales and dolphins), and that provide milk for their young. Mammals are divided into major groups (carnivores, primates, rodents, and marsupials to name just

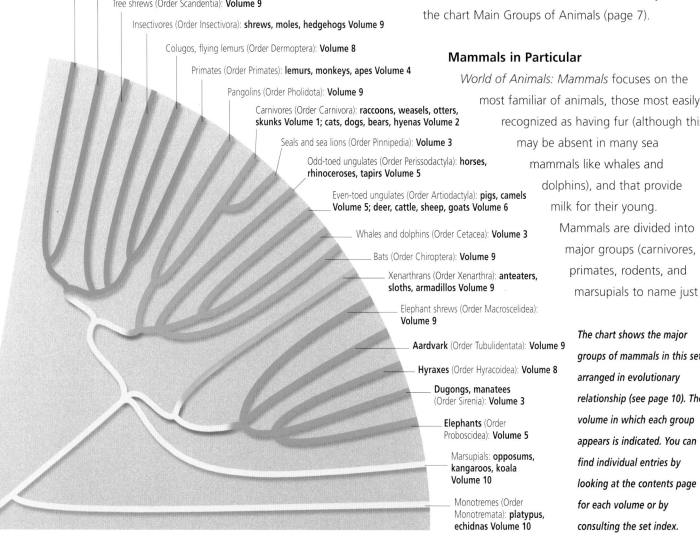

Rodents (Order Rodentia): **squirrels, rats, mice Volume 7; cavies, porcupines, chinchillas Volume 8**

Lagomorphs (Order Lagomorpha): **rabbits, hares, pikas Volume 8**

Tree shrews (Order Scandentia): **Volume 9**

Insectivores (Order Insectivora): **shrews, moles, hedgehogs Volume 9**

Colugos, flying lemurs (Order Dermoptera): **Volume 8**

Primates (Order Primates): **lemurs, monkeys, apes Volume 4**

Pangolins (Order Pholidota): **Volume 9**

Carnivores (Order Carnivora): **raccoons, weasels, otters, skunks Volume 1; cats, dogs, bears, hyenas Volume 2**

Seals and sea lions (Order Pinnipedia): **Volume 3**

Odd-toed ungulates (Order Perissodactyla): **horses, rhinoceroses, tapirs Volume 5**

Even-toed ungulates (Order Artiodactyla): **pigs, camels Volume 5; deer, cattle, sheep, goats Volume 6**

Whales and dolphins (Order Cetacea): **Volume 3**

Bats (Order Chiroptera): **Volume 9**

Xenarthrans (Order Xenarthra): **anteaters, sloths, armadillos Volume 9**

Elephant shrews (Order Macroscelidea): **Volume 9**

Aardvark (Order Tubulidentata): **Volume 9**

Hyraxes (Order Hyracoidea): **Volume 8**

Dugongs, manatees (Order Sirenia): **Volume 3**

Elephants (Order Proboscidea): **Volume 5**

Marsupials: **opposums, kangaroos, koala Volume 10**

Monotremes (Order Monotremata): **platypus, echidnas Volume 10**

The chart shows the major groups of mammals in this set arranged in evolutionary relationship (see page 10). The volume in which each group appears is indicated. You can find individual entries by looking at the contents page for each volume or by consulting the set index.

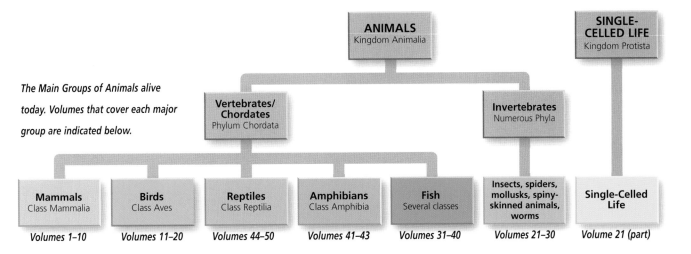

The Main Groups of Animals alive today. Volumes that cover each major group are indicated below.

| ANIMALS Kingdom Animalia | | | | | | SINGLE-CELLED LIFE Kingdom Protista |

| | Vertebrates/ Chordates Phylum Chordata | | | Invertebrates Numerous Phyla | | |

| Mammals Class Mammalia | Birds Class Aves | Reptiles Class Reptilia | Amphibians Class Amphibia | Fish Several classes | Insects, spiders, mollusks, spiny-skinned animals, worms | Single-Celled Life |
| Volumes 1–10 | Volumes 11–20 | Volumes 44–50 | Volumes 41–43 | Volumes 31–40 | Volumes 21–30 | Volume 21 (part) |

a few). All the major groups are shown on the chart on page 6. To help you find particular animals, a few familiar ones, such as sheep, goats, cats, and dogs, have been included in the chart.

Naming Mammals

To be able to discuss animals, names are needed for the different kinds. Most people regard tigers as one kind of animal and lions as another. All tigers look more or less alike. They breed together and produce young like themselves. This popular distinction between kinds of animals corresponds closely to the zoologists' distinction between species. All tigers belong to one species and all lions to another. The lion species has different names in different languages (for example, *Löwe* in German, *Simba* in Swahili), and often a single species may have several common names. For example, the North American mountain lion is also known as the cougar, puma, panther, and catamount.

Zoologists find it convenient to have internationally recognized names for species and use a standardized system of two-word Latinized names. The lion is called *Panthera leo* and the tiger *Panthera tigris*. The first word, *Panthera*, is the name of the genus (a group of closely similar species), which includes the lion and the tiger. The second word, *leo* or *tigris*, indicates the particular species within the genus. Scientific names are recognized all over the world. The scientific name is used whatever the language, even where the alphabet is different, as in Chinese or Russian. The convention allows for precision and helps avoid most confusion. However, it is also common for one species to apparently have more than one scientific name. That can be because a particular

species may have been described and named at different times without the zoologists realizing it was one species.

It is often necessary to make statements about larger groups of animals: for example, all the catlike animals or all the mammals. A formal system of classification makes this possible. Domestic cats are similar to lions and tigers, but not as similar as those species are to each other (for example, they do not roar). They are put in a different genus (*Felis*), but *Felis*, *Panthera*, and other catlike animals are grouped together as the family Felidae. The flesh-eating mammals (cats, dogs, hyenas, weasels, and so on), together with a few plant-eaters that are obviously related to them (such as pandas), are grouped in the order Carnivora. These and all the other animals that suckle their young are grouped in the class Mammalia. Finally, the mammals are included, with all other animals that have backbones (fish, amphibians, reptiles, and birds) and some other animals that seem to be related to them, in the Phylum Chordata.

Rank	Scientific name	Common name
Phylum	Chordata	Animals with a backbone
Class	Mammalia	All mammals
Order	Carnivora	Flesh-eaters/carnivores
Family	Felidae	All cats
Genus	*Panthera*	Big cats
Species	*leo*	Lion

The kingdom Animalia is subdivided into phylum, classes, orders, families, genera, and species. Above is the classification of the lion.

RODENTS

If the groups of mammals in this encyclopedia were given space according to their size, then the section on rodents would take up over four volumes. Over 40 percent of all living mammal species are rodents. There were 2,000 or so different species at the last count, with many more doubtless still waiting to be discovered. There are not only lots of different kinds of rodents, but some species are also mind-bogglingly abundant.

Despite their vast numbers and varied lifestyles, rodents are not especially diverse in appearance. There are a few odd-looking ones—the beavers, porcupines, capybaras, and flying squirrels, for example, are distinctive because of their special tail, long spines, large size, and gliding membranes respectively. But most rodent species are small enough to sit in the palm of your hand, and the vast majority are rat- or mouselike creatures with short legs and a coat color of buff, brown, or gray. Rodent tails are rather variable. Most are long, some short, and some virtually nonexistent. Some are furry; others naked. Most are roughly cylindrical, but some are flattened (either side-to-side or top-to-bottom), usually as an adaptation to

⊖ *Like most rodents Harris's antelope squirrel from southwestern America is small, brownish in color, and has a conspicuous tail. It is often seen above ground feeding on fruits and seeds.*

swimming. Rodents have five "fingers" on their front feet (although the thumb is sometimes reduced) and three, four, or five toes on the back feet. Most rodents walk on the soles of their feet and move by scampering or bounding. A few, such as the agoutis, run on the tips of their toes, more like antelope or pigs. Rodent claws vary to suit different lifestyles: They can be large and blunt for digging or small and sharp for

Classifying Rodents

Most mammal orders can be split quite comfortably into families and genera using obvious anatomical, physiological, and ecological characteristics. The rodents, however, are different. There are so many of them that it is helpful to use an extra level of classification. Until recently, rodents were divided into three main groups—the squirrel- and mouselike rodents (Sciuromorpha), the mouselike rodents (Myomorpha), and the cavy- and porcupinelike rodents (Caviomorpha). However, zoologists have now decided that squirrel- and mouselike rodents all belong in one group—the Sciurognathi. For good measure, the

Caviomorpha have been renamed Hystricognathi. The latter group is covered in Volume 8 of this set.

The groups are based on differences in the structure of the skulls, jaws, and teeth; and those differences are, to some extent, reflected geographically. With a few notable exceptions (including the North American porcupine), hystricognaths do not live in the northern temperate zone of North America or Eurasia. Sciurognaths, on the other hand, are more cosmopolitan. Such variations between groups are the result of over 35 million years of separate evolution in different parts of the world.

climbing. The
collared lemming grows an
extra broad, spadelike claw in
winter to help it burrow through snow. Several
semiaquatic rodents, such as beavers and water voles,
have fully or partially webbed toes.

Identity Parade

Most people would claim to recognize a rodent if they
saw one, but many would mistake shrews, moles, pikas,
and mouselike marsupials for rodents as well. In fact, the
only really reliable way to identify a rodent is to take a
look inside its mouth. Most rodents have fewer than 22
teeth, except the silvery mole rats (genus *Heliophobius*),
which have 28. The Australian water rat (*Hydromys
chrysogaster*), a predatory species, has only 12. Regardless
of number, rodent teeth are always arranged in a
distinctive pattern. At the front of the mouth are four

Who's Who among the Rodents?

Suborder: Sciurognathi—squirrel- and mouselike rodents: over 1,760 species in 11 families

Family: Sciuridae—tree, ground, and flying squirrels, chipmunks, prairie dogs, and marmots: about 270 species in 50 genera, including eastern chipmunk (*Tamias striatus*); American gray squirrel (*Sciurus carolinensis*); South African ground squirrel (*Xerus inauris*)

Family: Castoridae—beavers: 2 species in 1 genus, American beaver (*Castor canadensis*); Eurasian beaver (*C. fiber*)

Family: Aplodontidae—mountain beaver: 1 species in 1 genus (*Aplodontia rufa*)

Family: Pedetidae—springhare: 1 species in 1 genus (*Pedetes capensis*)

Family: Anomaluridae—scaly-tailed squirrels: 7 species in 3 genera, including Lord Derby's scaly-tailed squirrel (*Anomalurus derbianus*)

Family: Ctenodactylidae—gundis: 5 species in 4 genera, including North African gundi (*Ctenodactylus gundi*)

Family: Muridae—rats, mice, voles, hamsters, and gerbils: over 1,300 species in about 280 genera, including ship rat (*Rattus rattus*); house mouse (*Mus musculus*); bushveld gerbil (*Tatera leucogaster*) bank vole (*Clethrinomys glareolus*)

Family: Gliridae—dormice: 26 species in 8 genera, including edible dormouse (*Glis glis*); hazel dormouse (*Muscardinus avellanius*)

Family: Dipodidae—jumping mice, birch mice, jerboas, and kangaroo mice: 50 species in 15 genera, including Chinese jumping mouse (*Eozpus setchuanus*); Armenian birch mouse (*Sicista armenica*)

Family: Geomyidae—pocket gophers: 39 species in 5 genera, including northern pocket gopher (*Thomomys talpoides*)

Family: Heteromyidae—pocket mice, kangaroo mice, and kangaroo rats: 59 species in 5 genera, including desert pocket mouse (*Chaetopidus penicillatus*); Ord's kangaroo rat (*Dipodomys ordii*)

Suborder: Hystricognathi—cavy- and porcupinelike rodents: about 233 species in 17 familes

Family: Bathyergidae—mole rats: 12 species in 5 genera, including naked mole rat (*Heterocephalus glaber*)

Family: Hystricidae—Old World porcupines: 11 species in 3 genera, including crested porcupine (*Hystrix cresta*)

Family: Erethizontidae—New World porcupines: 12 species in 4 genera, including North American porcupine (*Erethizon dorsatum*)

Family: Petromuridae—dassie rat: 1 species in 1 genus (*Petromus typicus*)

Family: Thryonomyidae—cane rats: 2 species in 1 genus, lesser cane rat (*Thryonomys gregorianus*); greater cane rat (*T. swinderianus*)

Family: Chinchillidae—chinchillas: 6 species in 3 genera, including short-tailed chinchilla (*Chinchilla brevicaudata*)

Family: Dinomyidae—pacarana: 1 species in 1 genus (*Dinomys branickii*)

Family: Caviidae—guinea pigs, cavies, and maras: 14 species in 5 genera, including Brazilian guinea pig (*Cavia aperea*); Patagonian mara (*Dolichotis patagonum*)

Family: Hydrochaeridae—capybara: 1 species in 1 genus (*Hydrochaeris hydrochaeris*)

Family: Dasyproctidae—agoutis and acouchis: 13 species in 2 genera, including Mexican agouti (*Dasyprocta mexicana*)

Family: Agoutidae—pacas: 2 species in 1 genus, paca (*Agouti paca*); mountain paca (*A. taczanowskii*)

Family: Ctenomyidae—tuco-tucos: about 40 species in 1 genus, including tiny tuco-tuco (*Ctenomys minutus*)

Family: Octodontidae—rock rats and degus: 9 species in 6 genera, including moon-toothed degu (*Octodon lunatus*)

Family: Abrocomidae—chinchilla rats: 3 species in 1 genus, including ashy chinchilla rat (*Abrocoma cinerea*)

Family: Echimyidae—American spiny rats: about 70 species in 16 genera, including mouse-tailed spiny rat (*Proechimys myosarus*)

Family: Capromyidae—hutias: 12 species in 5 genera, including eared hutia (*Mesocapromys auritus*)

Family: Myocastoridae—coypu: 1 species in 1 genus (*Myocastor coypus*)

large, chisel-shaped incisors, two in the upper jaw and two in the lower. Behind the incisors (and in front of the molars) is a large gap. In many other mammal groups this gap is filled with more incisors and the large canine teeth, which are always absent in rodents. The gap, called the diastema, allows a rodent to close its mouth behind the incisors so that when it uses its front teeth for digging or

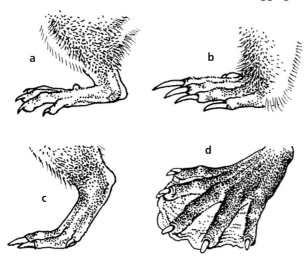

⊕ *Mice are plantigrade and walk on their palms and soles (a). Their nails may be elongated in some burrowing species, such as the Cape mole rats (b). Antelopelike species, such as the agouti (c), are digitigrade, carrying their weight on their fingers and toes. Rodents adapted for an aquatic life, like the beaver, have webbed hind feet (d).*

gnawing hard objects, such as wood or nut shells, it does not get a mouthful of unwanted dirt. Gnawing is one of the things rodents do best—the word rodent comes from the Latin verb *rodere*, which means "to gnaw." Gnawing is tough on teeth; and like all well-used tools, the rodents must keep their incisors sharp and somehow combat the wear and tear that goes with the job.

Origins

The first mammals appeared at the end of the Triassic period, about 220 million years ago. By the Jurassic period (205 to 146 million years ago) they had diverged into two distinct groups—the multituberculates and the pantotheres. The multituberculates were animals that had a number of striking similarities to modern rodents. For example, they had a similar arrangement of teeth (two incisors in the upper and lower jaw, separated from the cheek teeth by a gap). They ranged in size from mouse- to beaver-size and occupied a range of habitats on the ground and in the trees, just like modern rats and squirrels. But the multituberculates were not rodents, nor apparently were they even the ancestors of rodents. The group appears to have disappeared during the Eocene period, about 55 million years ago. However, fossil

⊜ *A South African ground squirrel nibbles on a melon. Manual dexterity is particularly well developed in squirrels, although other rodents make good use of their front paws for digging, grooming, and gathering food and nesting materials.*

Rodent Teeth

Rodent front teeth (incisors) are partly self-sharpening, being harder at the front than at the back. The hard front surface is coated with enamel, the shiny substance with which our own teeth are completely covered. As the rodent uses its incisors, the softer rear surface wears away faster, leaving a sharp edge of hard enamel at the front. The enamel on the incisors is often yellow or even bright orange.

To counteract the gradual wearing away at the tips of the teeth, rodent incisors are constantly growing. They are anchored deep in the animal's jaw, which makes them very strong. They have no nerves, except at the roots, so small chips and breaks do not hurt a rodent: Even if an incisor breaks off completely, the animal does not suffer pain, and the tooth can often grow back. However, the animal will be disadvantaged in the meantime, and problems can occur with the broken tooth's opposite number in the other jaw. With no opposing tooth to help wear it down, the remaining tooth grows out of control, gradually forming a long curve. If it is left unchecked, it will grow into a complete circle and ultimately pierce the rodent's head.

Behind the diastema, at the back of the rodent's mouth, are its cheek teeth. They are made up of alternating vertical layers of hard enamel and softer dentine and cement. In most rodent groups there are just molars, but in some mice, dormice, and squirrels there are premolars, too. In squirrels the premolars drop out as milk teeth and do not regrow.

The cheek teeth are complex and variable. Some are rooted, while others are nonrooted and grow continuously. The grinding surfaces are especially complex, with various cusps, loops, and infoldings of enamel and dentine. As with the incisors, the cheek teeth wear down at different rates, leaving the enamel layers standing up as sharp ridges. It is these patterns that often characterize different groups, and zoologists use the differences to classify rodent species into families and genera.

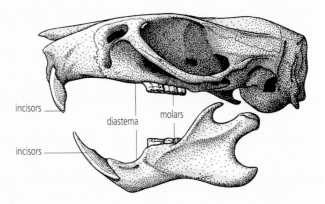

The skull of the ship rat, displaying the continuously growing gnawing incisors and chewing molars. There is a gap (diastema) left by the absence of canine and premolar teeth.

remains are proof that even in the very earliest stage of mammal evolution, the rodentlike form was a highly successful one. Part of the reason for the eventual decline of that ancient group was the rise of the true rodents. Along with almost all modern mammals, they evolved from pantothere stock, from the same branch as the rabbits and pikas. Some of the earliest unmistakably rodent fossils have been found in North America, but the group is thought to have first appeared in what is now Central Asia. The fossils illustrate that animals much like today's squirrels were scurrying around in dense Paleocene forests about 60 million years ago.

Expansion and Diversification

The real breakthrough for the rodents came about 30 million years ago, during the Oligocene period. About that time there was a sudden decline in mammal diversity, and many other previously successful orders went extinct. The rodents, however, thrived. They underwent a great expansion; and many modern families, including the squirrels, beavers, hamsters, dormice, cavies, and early rats and mice, became well established during that time. The next 25 million years or so saw rodents continue to diversify. Not every new group survived. Some notable extinct rodents include the 7-foot (2-m) long *Telicomys*, the largest rodent ever to have lived, and the bizarre horned gophers, which had one or two horns up to 12 inches (30 cm) long growing out of their nose!

Where Do Rodents Live?

Rodents are the only order of terrestrial mammals to occur naturally on four continents: Europe, Asia, the Americas, and Australia. Whales, seals, and bats have also achieved the distinction, but with the clear advantage that they can cross oceans by swimming or flying. Rodents are rather good at colonizing new places. Most are competent swimmers and are small enough to ride on rafts of floating debris in the ocean. This was probably the method by which rodents first came to such places as the Galápagos Islands. With a little help from humans they have also become established on the remotest islands. Even in Antarctica house mice thrive in and around international research stations and exploration

Why So Few Fossils?

For such a large and ancient group rodent fossils are surprisingly rare. A major reason for the dearth is that rodents and their bones are generally small and so are easily overlooked. Also, when rodents die, their corpses are rarely left undisturbed. Many are chewed and swallowed whole by larger animals or gnawed by smaller ones, which scatter the bones over a wide area. Only rarely will a dead rodent be immortalized as a complete fossil skeleton.

bases. Some islands, such as those in the Caribbean, are populated by the descendants of rodents that were stranded there millions of years ago—before the islands were separated from the mainland. Island species tend to evolve rapidly, and the Caribbean is home to many unique rodents, such as hutias. Such isolated species are vulnerable to extinction; many have been lost since the islands were colonized by people.

Within their vast distribution rodents have conquered almost every conceivable habitat except the open sea. Many live on the ground, while some—such as the blind mole rats—live almost

Octodonts (Octodontidae)
Spiny rats (Echimyidae)
Coypu (Myocastoridae)
Hutias (Capromyidae)
Tuco-tucos (Ctenomyidae)
Chinchilla rats (Abrocomidae)
Pacarana (Dinomyidae)
Chinchillas and viscachas (Chinchillidae)
New World porcupines (Erethizontidae)
Agoutis and acouchis (Dasyproctidae)
Pacas (Agoutidae)
Cavies (Caviidae)
Capybara (Hydrochaeridae)
African mole rats (Bathyergidae)
Dassie rat (Petromuridae)
Cane rats (Thryonomyidae)
Old World porcupines (Hystricidae)
Gundis (Ctenodactylidae)
Pocket gophers (Geomyidae)
Pocket mice (Heteromyidae)
Beavers (Castoridae)
Rats and mice (Muridae)
Jerboas (Dipodidae)
Springhare (Pedetidae)
Dormice (Myoxidae)
Mountain beaver (Aplodontidae)
Squirrels (Sciuridae)
Scaly-tailed squirrels (Anomaluridae)

Sciurognaths

Hystricognaths

EOCENE

PALEOCENE

55   34   million years ago

⊖ *Evolutionary tree based on relationships revealed by molecular techniques, with the branch lengths proportional to genetic similarities. Here, rodents are divided into two main groups, the Sciurognaths (squirrel- and mouselike rodents) and Hystricognaths (cavy- and porcupinelike rodents).*

→ *The bushveld gerbil has a ratlike appearance. It inhabits sandy plains, savannas, and woodlands. Its burrows may be dug up to 3 feet (1 m) underground.*

permanently under it. Lemmings and several voles spend months at a time in tunnels under the snow. Some rodents, notably members of the squirrel and dormouse families, are adapted to life in the trees, while the flying squirrels use the trees to launch themselves into the air. Beavers and muskrats spend as much time in water as they do on land, and kangaroo rats, gerbils, and gundis survive in places where there seems to be no water at all. There are specialized rodents living in deserts and forests, mountains and rivers, savanna and tundra, and generalized species that can make a successful living almost anywhere as the ubiquitous companions of human beings.

Lifestyles

The social lives of rodents range from solitary and fiercely territorial to utterly interdependent. Adult lemmings can hardly bear each other's company long enough to mate, and they eject their own offspring from their home range as soon as they are weaned. By contrast, naked mole rats are social in the extreme. Like honeybees, which cooperate as a hive and willingly sacrifice their lives for each other because they are so closely related, naked mole rats work selflessly for the good of their family. Most individuals are kept so busy caring for the colony, especially the single breeding queen mole rat and her babies, that they never get the chance to breed themselves. But because the colony is so inbred, helping rear their siblings, nephews, and nieces is genetically as worthwhile as having young of their own.

In between these two extremes are numerous variations on sociality. For example, beavers live in monogamous pairs, in which both the male and female help rear the family. House mice are polygynous—a single dominant male mates with several females in his territory and leaves them all to raise their offspring alone. Ship rat societies are dominated by females, while in prairie dogs the males sometimes team up to defend a coterie of shared females and young. Wood mice are solitary and territorial during the summer, but seek out company in winter, when shared body heat is the best way to survive.

Reproduction

Rodents are infamously fast breeders. The reproductive potential of mice and voles, for example, is such that a single pair could in theory multiply to over 10,000 animals in the space of a year. In reality that never happens, since relatively few animals live long enough to breed themselves. However, fast breeders have an advantage over other animals when it comes to colonizing new areas or recovering from population crashes. Animals that specialize in this kind of rapid-fire reproductive effort are known as "R strategists," while those that breed more slowly, investing more time in each offspring (to increase the proportion that survive) are called "K strategists." There are a number of K strategist rodents whose good parenting and slow and steady approach to reproduction are often overshadowed by the spectacular "boom and bust" antics of their relatives. The South American agouti, for example, rarely has more than one baby at a time and spends up to eight months rearing it, while the primitive mountain beaver lavishes prolonged parental care on just one very small litter a year. Other species have litters of eight to 10 young several times in quick succession during the breeding season.

The Old World mice and rats (subfamily Murinae) are now familiar the world over, since they include the three most abundant mammalian species that live in close

Rodents in the Food Chain

Human experience of rodents as pests of stored food means that we often tend to think of rodents as consumers of food as opposed to being food themselves. But the sad fate of most rodents is that they are eaten by something sooner or later. Rodents are killed by the million every day, and in most species there is very little an individual animal can do about it except hide whenever possible and breed so prolifically that it will always have descendants to take its place. Many predatory birds and mammals depend entirely on a diet of rodents and sometimes on just one or two species. For example, populations of Arctic foxes and snowy owls tend to fluctuate in accordance with lemming numbers. In good lemming years the foxes and owls do well; but following a crash, many will starve to death. Humans eat rodents, too, and in South America cavies are reared for food. The edible dormouse was considered a particular delicacy by the Romans and is still eaten in large numbers by country people in southeastern Europe.

association with us: the house mouse, brown rat, and ship rat. They are called "commensal" animals, and thanks to their unwelcome partnership with people these species have spread all around the world from their native Asia in cargoes transported overland or by sea. All three species are serious pests of stored food and carry diseases that can potentially infect humans. Most infamous is the bubonic plague, outbreaks of which have killed hundreds of millions of people throughout recorded history. Rodent populations around the world still serve as reservoirs of plague. Other rodent-borne diseases include typhus and Rocky Mountain tick fever (transmitted via blood-sucking ticks), bacterial infections like leptospirosis or Weil's disease, and viral diseases such as lassa fever and rabies.

Love-Hate Relationship

While house mice, brown rats, and ship rats are by far the most widespread rodent pests, other species can, and do, create considerable problems in localized areas. The blind mole rats of southeastern Europe and Central Asia, for example, inflict serious damage without ever emerging from their burrows. They spend their lives underground, constructing labyrinthine foraging tunnels under cultivated fields, from where they gnaw the roots of valuable crops. Along with American prairie dogs, they have earned the wrath of farmers for the threat their burrows pose to machinery and livestock. Certain dormice, squirrels, and chipmunks can also be a nuisance in houses, gardens, and parks; but not all human-rodent

⊕ *A female bank vole with young that are just over a week old. Soon their eyes will open, and within a few weeks the offspring will have families of their own.*

relations are hostile. House mice and brown rats have been bred in captivity since Victorian times, and there are now several hundred recognized strains of fancy rats and mice kept by devoted enthusiasts all over the world. Keeping hamsters and gerbils as pets is a more recent development, since the 1930s, which arose from spare research or zoo animals. Many rodents become valuable laboratory animals and have contributed immeasurably to groundbreaking and often life-saving research in certain areas of physiology, genetics, and pharmacology.

SQUIRREL-LIKE AND MOUSELIKE RODENTS

There are 11 families of squirrel-like and mouselike rodents gathered together into the suborder Sciurognathi. Five of them are large or distinctive enough to merit separate treatment in this volume (see introductions to beavers, squirrels, gundis, mice, and dormice); and two families contain only one living species apiece—the mountain beaver and the springhare. The remaining four families include animals such as the pocket mice and pocket gophers, the jerboas and kangaroo rats, and the bizarre scaly-tailed squirrels.

What Is a Sciurognath?

The word sciurognath means "squirrel-jaw" and describes the main distinguishing feature of an otherwise confusingly diverse group. The jaws of mammals are controlled by muscles called masseters. Rodent masseters are powerful: They not only open and close the jaws, but also provide a highly effective gnawing action. In nonsciurognath rodents, such as cavy- and porcupinelike rodents, gnawing is controlled by the deep masseter muscle, which is greatly enlarged. In the sciuromorphs (squirrels and beavers) it is the lateral masseter that is enlarged to perform that function. The rats and mice go one better: Both deep and lateral masseters are well developed, making them the best

⊕ *The skull of a marmot (shown left) demonstrates the primitive jaw musculature that is characteristic of squirrel-like rodents. The lateral masseter muscle (blue) extends in front of the eye onto the snout, moving the lower jaw forward during gnawing. The deep masseter muscle (red) is short and is used only in opening and closing the animal's jaw.*

⊕ *A meadow jumping mouse drinks from a puddle. Like all jumping mice, it will spend over half the year in hibernation, from October through April.*

gnawers of all. The way the muscles operate affects the action of the jaws and results in different jawbone shapes, which are part of the basis for classifying rodents.

The structure of their jaw muscles apart, members of this suborder appear to have little in common. In the 35 million years since they evolved away from the other rodents of the suborder Hystricognathi they have had plenty of time to adapt physically and ecologically to the full range of rodent habitats and lifestyles.

Rodent Diets

Plant material makes up the bulk of the diet of most sciurognaths. Nuts, seeds, fruit, leaves, and shoots contain carbohydrates and fats, both of which are important in fueling the active lifestyle of these diverse animals. Most sciurognaths are fast-moving, agile animals that breed rapidly and so need to eat plenty. The majority of species will supplement a basic vegetarian diet with animal protein in the form of insects and other invertebrates, eggs, and even small birds and other animals. Usually there will be opportunist snacks found in the course of foraging for other things, but a few species, such as the frog-eating Australian water rat, are active predators.

Climbers and Burrowers

Several groups of sciurognaths are excellent climbers, specialized for life in the trees. Tree squirrels, scaly-tailed squirrels, dormice, and several murid mice are all excellent climbers, with well-developed abdominal and shoulder muscles, feet and claws adapted for gripping, and a tail that makes a useful counterbalance when moving along narrow branches. The ultimate adaptation to arboreal life is shown by the flying and scaly-tailed squirrels, which are able to glide from tree to tree and never have to come down to the ground.

Among more down-to-earth members of the suborder are the kangaroo rats and mice and the "two-footed" mice—jerboas, birch mice, and jumping mice. All of them live on the ground and bounce around on their hind legs like miniature kangaroos. Their hind feet are powerful enough to launch them up to 30 times their own body length in a single bound, and their extremely long tails help provide stability in midleap. These

Who's Who among the Sciurognathi?

Family: Sciuridae—tree, ground, and flying squirrels, chipmunks, prairie dogs, and marmots: about 270 species in 50 genera, including eastern chipmunk (*Tamias striatus*); American gray squirrel (*Sciurus carolinensis*); European marmot (*Marmota marmota*)

Family: Castoridae—beavers: 2 species in 1 genus, American beaver (*Castor canadensis*); Eurasian beaver (*C. fiber*)

Family: Aplodontidae—mountain beaver: 1 species in 1 genus (*Aplodontia rufa*)

Family: Pedetidae—springhare: 1 species in 1 genus (*Pedetes capensis*)

Family: Anomaluridae—scaly-tailed squirrels: 7 species in 3 genera, including Lord Derby's scaly-tailed squirrel (*Anomalurus derbianus*)

Family: Ctenodactylidae—gundis: 5 species in 4 genera, including North African gundi (*Ctenodactylus gundi*)

Family: Muridae—rats, mice, voles, hamsters, and gerbils: over 1,300 species in about 280 genera, including house mouse (*Mus musculus*); ship rat (*Rattus rattus*); muskrat (*Ondanta zibethicus*); Australian water rat (*Hydromys chrysogaster*); Ehrenberg's mole rat (*Nannospalax ehrenbergi*)

Family: Gliridae—dormice: 26 species in 8 genera, including edible dormouse (*Glis glis*); hazel dormouse (*Muscardinus avellanius*)

Family: Dipodidae—jumping mice, birch mice, jerboas, and kangaroo mice: 50 species in 15 genera, including meadow jumping mouse (*Zapus hudsonius*); Armenian birch mouse (*Sicista armenica*)

Family: Geomyidae—pocket gophers: 39 species in 5 genera, including northern pocket gopher (*Thomomys talpoides*)

Family: Heteromyidae—pocket mice, kangaroo mice, and kangaroo rats: 59 species in 5 genera, including desert pocket mouse (*Chaetopidus penicillatus*); bannertail kangaroo rat (*Dipodomys spectabilis*)

adaptations are taken to the extreme in the desert-dwelling jerboas, whose hind feet are half the length of the body. The soles of the feet have a fringe of hair that gives the jerboa extra grip on loose sand and prevents its feet from sinking in.

Other terrestrial sciurognaths use such regular routes for getting around that over time they create obvious tracks and runways through dense vegetation. Social and territorial species regularly mark these runways with scent and droppings that advertise their presence and communicate personal information to other individuals passing the same route. In cold temperate climates, where the ground is covered in snow for part of the year, ground-dwelling rodents such as voles, lemmings, and gophers create tunnels in the snow in order to move around at ground level.

Many ground-dwelling sciurognaths live in burrows. The burrow can be a short, simple tube dug straight into a bank and used to shelter just one animal. But other burrow systems include huge underground networks of tunnels linking chambers used for sleeping, rearing offspring, hibernating, storing food, and excreting. The burrow provides a home for whole colonies. Ground squirrel and springhare burrows often have emergency entrances that drop straight through the roof of tunnels; those of water voles and water rats have entrances underwater. The tunnels of various species are often sealed with wads of vegetation or loose soil as a security measure, and prairie dogs build entrance cones as a precaution against flooding. Pocket gophers and mole rats may spend their entire lives underground. Animals adapted to a life of underground burrowing are called "fossorial." Typical fossorial traits are a cylindrical body, short, powerful legs, large claws or enlarged, protruding incisor teeth (used for digging), a thick skull, velvety fur, small ears, and reduced eyes. The blind mole rats have even given up their eyes altogether—sight being irrelevant in the darkness of their underground world.

Useful Pockets

Sciurognath rodents do not wear trousers, but several have pockets! Pocketed or pouched species include chipmunks and other squirrels, pouched rats, hamsters, gophers, and pocket mice. The pockets are dry pouches inside the animals' cheeks, which can expand to grotesque proportions to hold large quantities of food or other materials. In squirrels, hamsters, and pouched rats the pockets open inside the mouth, while in the pocket mice and gophers they are external. With the help of these convenient shopping bags a rodent can feed rapidly, stuffing food into its pouches to be carried away and

⊕ *A bannertail kangaroo rat forages for food. With the help of large pouches the rodent can rapidly stuff its cheeks with food, which is then carried off and either stored or eaten in a safer place elsewhere.*

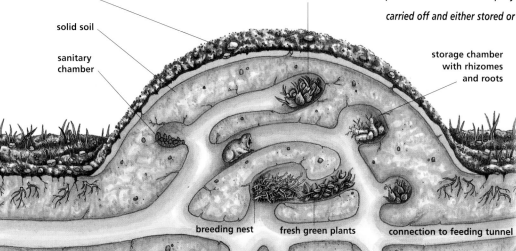

soft soil
solid soil
sanitary chamber
storage chamber with bulbs
storage chamber with rhizomes and roots
breeding nest
fresh green plants
connection to feeding tunnel

⊖ *The breeding mound of Ehrenberg's mole rat. Each animal makes its own system of tunnels, which may be up to 1,150 feet (350 m) long. Underground food storage chambers have been known to hold as much as 31 pounds (14 kg) of vegetables.*

eaten in safety somewhere less exposed. Often food is carried away and stashed: A single animal may amass huge stores—often well over 100 pounds (45 kg) and sometimes even twice that amount—of seeds and other nonperishable foods in a personal larder. Pouchless rodents store food by collecting small amounts at a time.

Hibernation and Estivation

The sciurognaths include some of the world's sleepiest mammals. Like storing food, prolonged periods of deep, torpid sleep are an adaptation to seasonal shortages. Rodents such as dormice, jumping mice, many ground squirrels, and sometimes hamsters can hibernate for anything up to nine months of the year. During deep hibernation an animal's body temperature drops well below normal (almost to freezing point in some dormice), and metabolic processes slow right down. It saves a lot of energy; but even so, a long hibernation requires the animal to be fat and healthy in the first place. Estivation is the summertime equivalent and usually happens during dry seasons or droughts when food is in short supply.

⊖ *The scaly-tailed squirrels seem to be only distantly related to true squirrels. Little is known about their habits, since they live in remote parts of the African rain forest and are nocturnal.*

Scaly-Tailed Squirrels—Odd Ones Out

By far the strangest group of squirrel-like rodents are the scaly-tailed squirrels, whose family name, Anomaluridae, means "peculiar ones." They are an ancient group of arboreal rodents whose members have independently evolved the ability to glide. Despite their outward appearance, they may not be closely related to squirrels at all, and they are sometimes placed in a different suborder. The gliding membranes of scaly-tailed squirrels are supported by a stiffening rod, made of cartilage, that grows from the elbow joint. These curious squirrels also have a series of large, overlapping scales on the underside of their tail that aid climbing and landing by gripping the bark of trees, a bit like extra claws. In addition to these peculiarities the scaly-tailed squirrels do not have the normal sciurognath arrangement of teeth and skull.

Common name Springhare
(springhaas)

Scientific name *Pedetes capensis*

Family	Pedetidae
Order	Rodentia
Size	Length head/body: 14–17 in (36–43 cm); tail length: 14.5–19 in (37–48 cm)
Weight	6.6–8.8 lb (3–4 kg)
Key features	Kangaroolike rodent with very small forelimbs and long back feet; short snout; large eyes; big, leaf-shaped ears; fur thin and soft, reddish-brown to buff, paler on belly; end of tail has big black brush
Habits	Generally nocturnal; digs burrows; lives alone but feeds in groups; hops on hind legs like a kangaroo
Breeding	Three litters of 1 (occasionally 2) young born at any time of year after gestation period of 80 days. Weaned at 7 weeks; sexually mature at 2–3 years. May live up to 19 years in captivity, probably many fewer in the wild
Voice	Soft grunts and high-pitched piping calls
Diet	Roots, bulbs, and grasses; leaves and seeds of other plants, including crops; occasionally insects such as locusts and beetles
Habitat	Desert and semidesert with dry sandy soils
Distribution	Two populations: 1 in Kenya and Tanzania; the other in arid and semiarid parts of Angola, southern Democratic Republic of Congo, Namibia, South Africa, Botswana, Zimbabwe, and southern Mozambique
Status	Population: unknown, probably tens of thousands; IUCN Vulnerable. Still abundant, but declining rapidly; hunted for food and as a crop pest

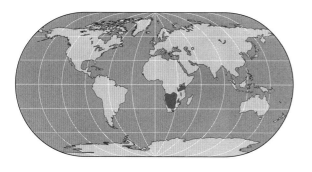

Springhare

Pedetes capensis

The mammal equivalent of a jack-in-the-box, the springhare is a very unusual rodent. Its huge back legs allow it to hop like a kangaroo, while its forepaws are adapted for digging.

THE SPRINGHARE IS SIMILAR in size and some of its behavior to a regular hare or jackrabbit. Were it not for the fact that it lives in Africa and not Australia, you could be forgiven for thinking it was a kind of small, bushy-tailed kangaroo. In fact, it is neither a hare nor a kangaroo, but belongs to its own exclusive family of rodents and apparently has no close relatives.

Hops and Bounds

Like kangaroos, the springhare has large, powerful hind legs and greatly elongated hind feet. They each have four toes, but the outside toe is small and does not carry any weight. The three remaining toes are large, especially the middle one, and the claws are so broad they look like little hooves. In contrast, the front legs are small and more typically rodentlike. They have five toes, each of which bears a long, curved claw that serves not as a weapon, but for digging. When moving slowly, for example, while feeding, springhares adopt a rabbitlike gait. When speed is required, they use just their hind legs to bound along like a kangaroo. They also sleep sitting up on their haunches with their head and forelegs tucked in.

Springhares are accomplished burrowers. Burrow systems allow shelter from heat, cold, and from predators, and provide a place to rear young. Burrows typically consist of several chambers and interconnected tunnels, with an average of nine or 10 entrances. Springhares dig in sandy soils, which drain easily, and most burrowing happens in the wet season, when the soil is not so hard. There are two types of entrance to a springhare burrow: One is gently sloping and is often plugged with loose earth to deter interest from potential predators. The

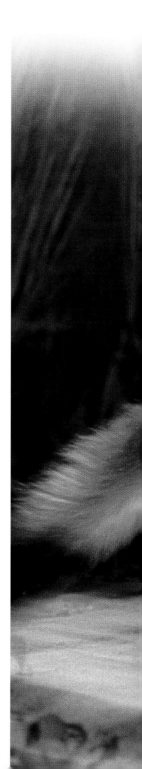

other kind is designed for rapid access or exit and opens directly onto the roof of a tunnel. If a springhare is disturbed while feeding, it will immediately bound (on two legs) to its nearest tunnel entrance and jump straight in. Springhares can appear equally suddenly and often emerge from their burrows with a great leap into the air. It may seem strange for the animal to draw attention to itself in this way; but by appearing so abruptly, the springhare can catch potential predators unawares.

Many Enemies

The springhare's main predators include wild and domestic cats and dogs, owls, pythons, and humans. Springhares are not hunted for their fur, which is extremely thin and not considered valuable; but their meat is a staple in the diets of several native tribes in southern Africa. In addition, many springhares are killed as pests when they turn their foraging attentions to cereal and groundnut crops.

Adult springhares generally live alone in a burrow, but they feed alongside each other quite amicably in groups of half a dozen or more. Each springhare will use several different burrows within its home range, and feeding usually takes place close to an entrance. Only in droughts when food is hard to find will springhares venture farther afield, sometimes wandering many miles in search of fresh grass.

Female springhares can give birth three times a year, but litters are small, usually consisting of just one large baby weighing up to 10 ounces (280 g). The youngsters are well cared for and reach independence at about 14 weeks. However, full maturity takes much longer, and most springhares are well into their third year before they manage to breed.

⊕ The springhare is still quite common despite being frequently hunted by humans. It is a vital resource for the Bushmen of southwestern Africa, who eat its meat, make its skin into garments, and even smoke its fecal pellets.

Common name Desert pocket mouse (coarse-haired pocket mouse)

Scientific name *Chaetodipus penicillatus*

Family Heteromyidae

Order Rodentia

Size Length head/body: 3–5 in (8–12 cm); tail length: 3–5.5 in (8–14 cm)

Weight 0.5–1.5 oz (14–43 g)

Key features Buff-gray mouse with pale underside; fur coarse; cheek pouches open on either side of mouth

Habits Nocturnal; burrow-dwelling; solitary

Breeding Litters of 1–8 young born in spring and summer after gestation period of 23 days. Weaned at 3–4 weeks; sexually mature within a few weeks. Closely related *C. fallax* has lived 8 years in captivity; life span in the wild likely to be much shorter

Voice Generally silent

Diet Seeds and other plant material; occasionally insects, grubs, and other small invertebrates

Habitat Sparsely vegetated sandy desert

Distribution Desert regions of Utah, Nevada, California, Arizona, and New Mexico; central to northwestern Mexico

Status Population: unknown, but probably millions

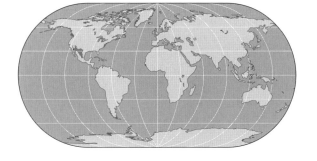

Desert Pocket Mouse

Chaetodipus penicillatus

The desert pocket mouse is one of about 35 species of pocket mouse, all of which look quite similar and are told apart by differences in their fur and their way of life. As its name suggests, the species is a true sandy desert specialist.

POCKET MICE BELONG TO THE same family of rodents as the kangaroo mice and kangaroo rats, but they lack the enlarged hind legs and hopping gait that make their relatives so distinctive. Instead, they move around with a typical mouselike scamper on legs that are a similar length. Pocket mice are exclusively New World animals, and most species are confined to Central America and the western United States.

One of 14 coarse-haired pocket mouse species, the desert pocket mouse has rough fur, especially on its rump, where the hairs are almost bristly. The species also bears a crest of darker hairs along the top of its tail, which ends in a sparse tuft of long hairs.

A Pocketful of Seeds

While other pocket mouse species favor rocky habitats or grassland areas with dense vegetation cover, the desert species makes do with the sparsest vegetation and loose, sandy soils. The desert habitat is harsh and unpredictable. Droughts may last years, but sudden rains can transform an arid wilderness into a garden of plenty within days. The seeds produced in these brief periods last a long time in the dry, sandy conditions. Desert pocket mice collect the seeds by sifting through the sand under desert plants, tucking what they find into large external cheek pouches. The pouches are lined with fur and can be turned inside out for cleaning. By stuffing their cheek pouches, like filling their pockets (hence the name), pocket

stabilize the tunnels, which are constructed in loose, sandy soil and are otherwise prone to collapse. When digging a new burrow, the pocket mouse is careful to scatter the excavated soil over a wide area, since a mound of soil at the entrance might give away its location.

⬆ *A desert pocket mouse forages next to cactus leaves in the dry desert. It is able to extract enough water from its food to survive without drinking.*

mice can transport many days' worth of food in a single journey to a safe place for storage.

Like many small desert animals, pocket mice avoid the worst of the heat by spending the day underground. They forage only at night, returning to their burrows in the morning and blocking the entrance with loose soil. Inside the burrow the air remains quite cool and humid throughout the day. During especially hot, cold, or dry weather desert pocket mice can spend many days, even weeks, inside their burrows, surviving on stored food.

Pocket mice are fairly particular about burrow sites. They prefer to build entrances in the shelter of a plant or rock, which provides some shade and also cover from predatory eyes. The deep roots of desert plants also help

Strategy for a Poor Season

Desert pocket mice breed according to the availability of food. In a good year a female can rear up to 20 young in three litters, while in poor seasons she may only manage one litter. In difficult times up to 70 percent of females will make no attempt to breed at all. By moderating their reproductive effort in this way, pocket mice manage to considerably reduce infant mortality. The majority of young born in a year will survive at least until the next spring. Under ideal (captive) conditions desert pocket mice might live as long as eight years, but in the wild their survival is highly dependent on the rains. However, these are unreliable, and every few years there will be a poor growing season and a subsequent die-off of pocket mice.

Common name Ord's kangaroo rat

Scientific name *Dipodomys ordii*

Family	Heteromyidae
Order	Rodentia
Size	Length head/body: 4–4.5 in (10–11 cm); tail length: 5–6 in (13–15 cm)
Weight 1.3–1.9 oz (37–54 g)	
Key features	Small rat with large head, large black eyes, and rounded ears; hind legs and feet much longer than in front; very long tail with dark stripe along the top ending in tuft of long hairs; fur rich gold above, white below, with white band across tops of hind legs
Habits	Nocturnal; lives alone in shallow burrow system
Breeding	Up to 3 litters of 1–6 young born in spring or summer after gestation period of 29–30 days. Weaned at 3–4 weeks; sexually mature at 2 months. May live up to 10 years in captivity, usually many fewer in the wild
Voice	Usually silent, sometimes uses foot drumming for communication
Diet	Seeds and grains
Habitat	Dry scrub, grassland, and desert
Distribution	Southwestern Canada (Alberta and Saskatchewan) to northern-central Mexico
Status	Population: abundant

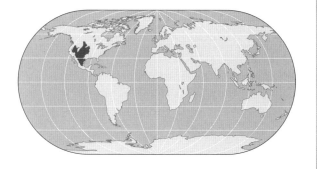

Ord's Kangaroo Rat

Dipodomys ordii

Like its close relatives the kangaroo mice and pocket mice, Ord's kangaroo rat has large cheek pouches for storing food. The feature is just one adaptation, demonstrated by this desert specialist to life in arid zones .

AS THEIR NAME SUGGESTS, KANGAROO rats have powerful back legs and move around by hopping. They can leap up to 6.5 feet (2 m), or well over 10 times their body length, in a single bound. The front legs are small by comparison, and the kangaroo rat uses them only for slow walking. Most of the time the front paws are used for sorting food and grooming.

Seed Stash

Ord's kangaroo rat is one of several species that survive in the deserts of western North America by feeding on the seeds that accumulate in the dry, sandy soils. Like pocket mice, kangaroo rats collect seeds in large, fur-lined cheek pouches and stash them away in underground burrows.

The burrows are shallow, presumably because the sandy soils are somewhat unstable. They contain nesting and food storage chambers, which are linked by interconnecting tunnels. A kangaroo rat's burrow is most definitely its castle, and the rather cute-looking animal will fight with surprising ferocity to defend its territory. Fights usually involve boxing with the front paws, kicking with the powerful hind legs, and scuffing sand into the opponent's face. Scent is known to play an important part in marking out a territory. A gland between the kangaroo rat's shoulders oozes an oily substance that the rat spreads liberally around its territory by wriggling in the sand. Kangaroo rats also use foot drumming as a means of alerting other individuals to their presence.

Survival Specialists

Kangaroo rats provide a textbook example of how to survive in arid conditions. Their success depends on a whole range of physiological and behavioral adaptations to help them keep cool and conserve water. They do not drink, and their food consists only of dry seeds and grains. In fact, their diet seems impossibly dry—scientists have estimated that the average kangaroo rat consumes only a tenth of the water it needs to survive. But the animal makes up the difference from water produced during the metabolism of its food. By creating and saving so-called "metabolic water," it compensates for the lack of moisture in its diet. It also makes use of dew on leaves at night.

Even so, making water takes energy, and so there is still precious little to waste. The kangaroo rat conserves what moisture it has by staying in its cool burrow during the day, therefore avoiding the need to sweat. Its ultraefficient kidneys produce urine that is four times more concentrated than a human's, and its droppings are almost completely dry. The kangaroo rat avoids losing water from its lungs by having a cool nose within which water vapor condenses before it can be breathed out.

Ord's kangaroo rat is one of the more widespread species of *Dipodomys*. Several of its close relatives are threatened by habitat destruction as people develop marginal land around deserts for agriculture or urban use.

↑ *An Ord's kangaroo rat searches for seeds in the sand. Kangaroo rats are known to compete with smaller pocket mice for food where their territories overlap.*

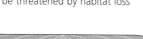

Common name Northern pocket gopher (western pocket gopher)

Scientific name *Thomomys talpoides*

Family	Geomyidae
Order	Rodentia
Size	Length head/body: 5–7 in (12–19 cm); tail length: 1.5–3 in (4–8 cm)

Weight 2–6 oz (57–170 g). Male up to twice as heavy as female

Key features Robust body with short legs and large, long-clawed feet; tail short with naked tip; very thick neck and massive head, with small eyes and ears; lips close behind prominent incisor teeth; coat short and silky, any shade of brown from near-black to creamy white

Habits Solitary; aggressive; burrowing; mostly nocturnal

Breeding Single litter of 1–10 (usually 3–5) young born in spring after gestation period of 18 days. Weaned at 40 days; sexually mature at 1 year. May live up to 4 years in the wild, probably similar in captivity, although not normally kept for very long

Voice Generally silent

Diet Roots, bulbs, tubers, stems, and leaves of various plants, including many crops

Habitat Prairie grassland, forest, agricultural land, and anywhere else with soil suitable for burrowing

Distribution Southwestern Canada and western U.S.

Status Population: abundant. Some subspecies may be threatened by habitat loss

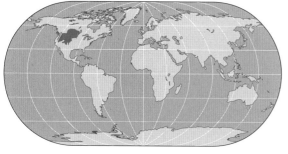

 SEE ALSO Mouse, Desert Pocket 7:22

Northern Pocket Gopher

Thomomys talpoides

Pocket gophers are the most ancient living family of burrowing rodents. They have spent over 36 million years perfecting the art of excavation.

THE NORTHERN POCKET GOPHER spends most of its life in a private system of tunnels—some shallow, some up to 10 feet (3 m) deep. The deep burrows include sleeping and food storage chambers, and the shallow ones are used for foraging. Burrow entrances are usually sealed with a plug of loose earth but are marked by a distinctive fan-shaped heap of excavated soil. In winter the tunnels extend out of the ground and into the layer of overlying snow. The gophers line their snow tunnels with soil, ridges of which can be seen crisscrossing the landscape after the spring thaw.

Most digging is done with the claws of the front feet; but when the gopher comes across a patch of compacted soil, it uses its front teeth

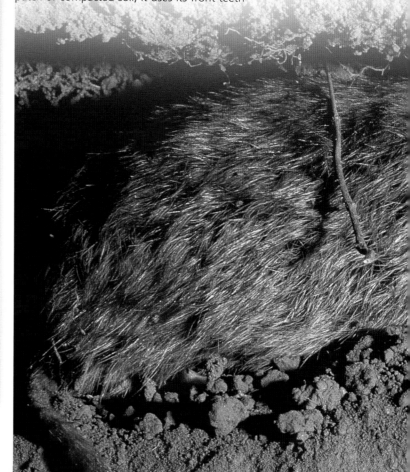

to gnaw its way through. The gopher's furry lips close behind the teeth so the animal can dig without getting dirt in its mouth. Even so, with such treatment and a diet of gritty roots, the gopher's incisor teeth are subjected to an immense amount of wear. Were it not for the fact that they grow continuously throughout the gopher's life, they would be eroded to nothing in the space of a few weeks.

Tails as Guides

Underground, pocket gophers can run forward and backward with almost equal speed. When going backward, the gopher uses its highly sensitive tail to feel its way along the tunnel. The tail tip is hairless and contains many nerves. The rest of the gopher's body is also sensitive to touch—the coat contains many special hairs that connect directly to nerves below the skin.

Male pocket gophers are considerably larger than females—a sure sign that size and strength are a factor in competing for mates. Gophers are aggressive animals and will fight over mates and territory. Most males carry serious scars from fighting, and the injuries inflicted are often fatal. Females will only permit males near their burrows in the mating season. During the rest of the year they will viciously repel intruders. The loose-fitting skin that allows gophers to turn easily in small spaces is equally useful in combat—it means that bites do not easily penetrate to the tissues beneath. Even when a gopher is held by the neck, it can still wriggle around and bite back.

Northern pocket gophers breed once a year. Maximum litter size is 10, but five is more normal. After two months the young gophers are fully weaned and independent, but face many dangers. Gophers dispersing from their mother's burrows are vulnerable to attack from carnivores, such as badgers and coyotes, and birds of prey. The northern pocket gopher is often persecuted because of its potential to do damage to crop plants. However, most control measures are only partially effective. Perhaps that is just as well because pocket gophers can also be highly beneficial, especially for grazing land. Their tunneling helps loosen and aerate the soil, improving drainage and encouraging the growth of herbaceous plants.

⊕ *Like their relatives the pocket mice, pocket gophers have large external cheek pouches in which they transport food. They do not appear to use the pockets for moving soil—that is shoved out of the tunnels using the feet, chin, and chest.*

The Beaver and Mountain Beaver Families

True beavers are semiaquatic rodents belonging to the family Castoridae. They are among the largest of the world's rodents, second only in size to the South American capybara. However, even today's species would be dwarfed by the giant beavers of the Pleistocene era, some of which weighed as much as 700 pounds (320 kg). The two living species—the American beaver and Eurasian beaver—are alike in behavior and outward appearance. A third species—the mountain beaver—is superficially similar, but not closely related. It is classified in a separate family of its own, the Aplodontidae.

What Is a Beaver?

True beavers are robust, short-legged animals, with a small head and a thick, powerful neck. Most distinctive is the flat, paddle-shaped tail, which is covered with large scales. There are five clawed toes on each foot. The forepaws are dexterous, and the hind feet are extra large with webbing between the toes. On land beavers move around with a rolling waddle or a bounding gallop; when swimming, they use their tail and hind feet for propulsion as they steer gracefully through the water.

The beaver's eyes, ears, and nostrils are located on the top of its head so that the animal can see, hear, breathe, and smell while swimming low in the water. It is therefore able to keep an eye on what is going on above

Family Castoridae (true beavers): 1 genus, 2 species

Castor American beaver (*C. canadensis*); Eurasian beaver (*C. fiber*)

Family Aplodontidae (mountain beaver): 1 genus, 1 species

Aplodontia (*A. rufa*)

water without drawing too much attention to itself. The nostrils close when diving, and the beaver blocks its throat with its tongue so it can gnaw and carry plant material without swallowing water. The beaver's eyes are protected under water by a transparent third eyelid, known as a nictitating membrane. Beavers have extremely large, chisel-shaped front teeth (incisors) and broad, flat cheek teeth used for grinding.

Lifestyle

The beaver's way of life is unique among wild mammals. Many animals build nests or dens in which to shelter and raise young, but in the beaver the behavior extends to the creation of an entire habitat. Using their incisors, beavers fell branches and small trees and use the timber to make large dams. The dam blocks the flow of a small stream, causing water to accumulate into a lagoon. Within the lagoon the beavers construct a lodge—a mound of branches, logs, and silt several feet (about 1 m) across within which they can shelter. Building and maintaining the lodge and dam are a team effort undertaken by a breeding pair and their older offspring. The beavers mark their territory using scent. Most activity takes place at night. Beavers are strictly vegetarian and feed mostly on plant stems and soft, woody material.

Where Do Beavers Live?

Beavers occur naturally throughout much of the Northern Hemisphere. Both the American and the Eurasian species have suffered as a result of trapping for fur. However,

 SEE ALSO Beaver, American 7:30; Capybara 8:48

⬅ When swimming fast, the semiaquatic beaver propels itself with powerful up-and-down thrusts of the tail.

⬇ Mountain beavers seldom appear above the ground. The rare image below shows the squat, thickset appearance of the elusive creature.

populations are now recovering from the low levels of the early 20th century. Eurasian beavers have been successfully reintroduced to several countries, including Belgium and the Netherlands. A small population is also due for release in Scotland. American beavers have been introduced to parts of Europe, and there are thriving populations in Finland in particular. While the two species will not successfully interbreed (they have a different number of chromosomes), there are concerns that the presence of the American beaver may harm the Eurasian beaver's chances of recolonizing parts of its former range.

The Mountain Beaver

The primitive North American rodent known as the mountain beaver, or sewellel, is the sole surviving member of the family Aplodontidae. It is only distantly related to the true beavers. It can swim, but lacks the beaver's paddle-shaped tail and does not share its relative's semiaquatic lifestyle. In fact, it lives in gopherlike burrows and collects much of its food (fleshy leaves, shoots, and soft wood) while climbing somewhat clumsily in the trees. However, the shape of the sewellel's body and head are superficially beaverlike, hence its common name. Mountain beavers are not restricted to mountains—in fact, they do not cope well with snow and rarely live at high altitudes. They are better suited to damp forests, especially plantations where there is plenty of fresh new growth. They are hardly ever seen and probably not numerous.

Common name American beaver (Canadian beaver)

Scientific name *Castor canadensis*

Family	Castoridae
Order	Rodentia
Size	Length head/body: 31–47 in (80–120 cm); tail length: 10–20 in (25–50 cm)

Weight 24–66 lb (11–30 kg)

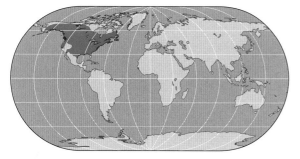

Key features Robust body with short legs and large, webbed hind feet; tail scaly, flattened, and paddlelike; small eyes and ears; coat dense and waterproof, light to rich dark brown

Habits	Lives in small territorial colonies of related animals; semiaquatic; fells small trees to build lodges and dams that are of great importance to wetland ecosystem; largely nocturnal
Breeding	Single litter of 1–9 (usually 2–4) young born in spring after gestation period of 100–110 days. Weaned at 3 months; sexually mature at 18–24 months. May live over 24 years in captivity, up to 24 in the wild
Voice	Hisses and grunts; also announces presence by slapping tail on water surface
Diet	Aquatic plants such as water lilies and leaves; also bark, twigs, roots, and other woody tissues of waterside trees and shrubs
Habitat	Lakes and streams among light woodland
Distribution	Canada, Alaska, and much of contiguous U.S.; introduced to parts of Finland
Status	Population: 6–12 million. Abundant—recovered well after serious decline due to excessive fur trapping in 18th and 19th centuries; regulated hunting still takes place

American Beaver

Castor canadensis

The industrious American beaver has helped shape the economic and ecological history of North America. Prodigious construction skills, a cooperative family life, and usefulness as a fur-bearing animal have given the rodent huge significance throughout its range.

AMERICAN BEAVERS ARE NATURALLY widespread, occurring from Alaska to northern Mexico. There are also thriving populations in Europe, especially in Finland, where the species was introduced following the decline of the native Eurasian beaver. Good beaver habitat consists of lightly wooded country dominated by species such as aspen, willow, and alder, all of which grow best in wet conditions. Water is vital to the beaver, which has a semiaquatic lifestyle.

Happy Families

Beaver colonies usually consist of one breeding pair along with their offspring of the past year or two. Beavers usually pair for life, and all members of the family help with chores such as maintaining the home (a lodge built of timber), watching over the babies, and gathering food. This kind of arrangement is close to the idealized human family, and it is one reason why beavers are regarded with affection by most people. Beaver family life is not without its trials, however, and young adults that have outstayed their welcome will eventually be driven out by their parents. Interactions with neighboring colonies are not necessarily amicable either: Members use scented heaps of dirt, twigs, and dung to mark out their territory and indulge in tail-slapping displays in the water to warn off intruders.

Where a beaver territory includes a suitable sheltered waterside bank, the family may set up home in a specially dug burrow. But if there is no natural site available, the resourceful beavers build one. First, they dam up a stream, creating

SEE ALSO Otter, North American River **1:**64; Wolf, Gray **2:**54; Bear, American Black **2:**90

a large pool in which they can construct an island of timber and silt. Within the mound is a spacious living chamber, the entrance to which is underwater. These "lodges" are excellent places to bring up young beavers, since they are protected from most predators by the surrounding moat of cold water.

Construction Workers

Among the mammals the architectural and construction skills of beavers are second only to those of humans. Beaver dams and lodges are large structures, made mostly of timber—branches, logs, and sometimes whole trees up to 40 inches (100 cm) in diameter! That is unusual, however, and most trees felled are less than 10 inches (25 cm) thick. They are felled close to the water's edge by the beaver's huge gnawing teeth, then towed through the water and wedged firmly into place with dexterous front paws. Lodges, dams, and burrows are not the beaver's only feats of engineering. In order to transport enough timber for building, the beavers often have to excavate substantial canals through areas that are either too shallow or weed-choked to accommodate large floating branches without snagging.

Once built, beaver dams require constant maintenance and repair, especially during

⊖ *The North American beaver is perfectly adapted to its semiaquatic lifestyle. Its fur is warm and waterproof, and it can close its ears and nose while diving underwater.*

Beaver Scent

The scents used by beavers to mark out their territory are produced in glands connected to the urinary tract. One of these scents is a substance unique to beavers and is known as castoreum. In the past castoreum was used to treat medical conditions including stomach cramps, ulcers, and various other aches and pains. The active ingredient that made these treatments effective is almost certainly salicin, a compound produced by willow trees. Salicin is the compound from which the common painkiller aspirin is derived. Beavers feeding on willow accumulate salicin in their body and use it in the production of scent. In recent times castoreum has become more commonly used as a base for perfumes.

spring, when many timbers are dislodged by fast-flowing melt water. A well-maintained dam will serve many generations of beavers, but they do not last indefinitely. Sooner or later the pool behind the dam becomes silted up, and the water will find an alternative route around the site, leaving the lodge high and dry. The resident beavers must then move on and begin again from scratch. The silted-up pools created in such a way eventually become willow thickets and lush meadows, replacing the woodland that once grew there. That offers opportunities for many species of insects, birds, and plants to live in an area where they would otherwise be absent. The beaver acts as a landscape architect, transforming the habitat. It is a good example of a keystone species on which many others depend for their survival.

Beavers do not hibernate, but in the north of their range they are seldom seen during winter. There is often a thick layer of ice and snow covering the pool, which effectively seals the beavers in. The silt in the thick lodge walls freezes solid, so that even if predators such as wolves and bears cross the ice, they are rarely able to break in. The beavers, however, can still come and go from the lodge by underwater entrances. During winter, when food is scarce, they can survive on plant material (mainly shoots and woody material) stored in special "caches" during the summer. The animals also have a reserve of fat stored in the tail, which helps them survive if spring comes late and food stocks run low.

During their winter confinement beavers live for several months without seeing true daylight. As result, their daily cycles of rest and activity are regulated by their own body clocks, rather than by the rising and setting of the sun. During these times they appear to

⊕ *The beavers' home is a large pile of mud and branches sited on a riverbank or in the middle of a lake. It contains different rooms, with a living chamber above the water level and sometimes a dining area nearer the water.*

switch from a regular 24-hour cycle to a longer one, something between 26 and 29 hours. Interestingly, the same happens with humans. People such as prisoners or experimental volunteers who live without natural light or artificial aids to telling the time develop a similar extended daily cycle and therefore often miscalculate the number of days they have been shut away.

Beaver Wars

The beaver's lustrous fur is soft, warm, and waterproof—qualities that are also greatly valued by humans. In the early colonial history of North America beaver trapping was so profitable that wars were fought over ownership of large areas of beaver habitat. Access to beaver skins was a major incentive to the exploration and opening up of the continent. Later, the fashion for felt top hats made from beaver fur encouraged still more trapping. Beavers were killed by the hundreds of thousands each year, and not surprisingly the population dwindled rapidly. Beavers are easy to

⬆ *Beavers only produce one small litter of kits each year. All members of the colony, which includes young of previous years, share tasks such as baby-sitting and providing the kits with solid food.*

⬅ *An American beaver building a dam. Although sometimes considered a nuisance by humans, dams in fact provide a natural filtration system that removes harmful impurities from the water. The large areas of wetlands that dams create also encourage greater biodiversity.*

find and are also easily trapped. By the early 20th century beavers had disappeared from much of their former range, and the species was in real danger of extinction. The loss of the beavers had enormous carry-over effects on entire wetland ecosystems. Without the beavers to build dams water drained rapidly from areas where it had formerly remained as pools. While excess water from heavy rainfall and spring thaws once spread gently over a wide area, in the absence of beavers it created raging torrents and flash floods.

Thankfully the danger was recognized in the nick of time, and legislation was put in place to preserve the remaining beaver stocks. Careful management has enabled numbers to recover, while allowing controlled trapping to continue. Beavers returned to much of their former range through recolonization, and other populations have been restocked artificially by bringing in beavers from elsewhere.

The reappearance of beavers is not always welcome, and there is an ongoing conflict between conservationists, trappers, and people who want to use the land for other purposes. Arable farmers claim that beaver activity harms their interests by flooding crop fields. Floods can also damage roads and other human infrastructure—one example of a situation in which commercial interests are at odds with ecological considerations. Establishing a compromise is one of the toughest challenges facing policymakers now and in the future.

The Squirrel Family

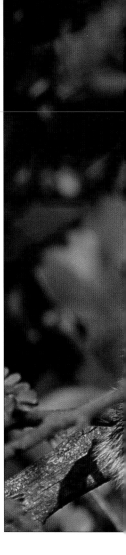

Squirrels are among the oldest rodents. In terms of their physiological form they have hardly changed in 30 million years. Fossil remains of members of the genus *Sciurus* (the same as the American gray and European red squirrels) have been found in rock deposits 25 million years old.

What Is a Squirrel?

The squirrels form the second largest family of rodents after the rats and mice. Typical tree squirrels have a prominent bushy tail; ground squirrels have only a small tail and coarser fur. The basic squirrel body is unspecialized and distinguished by a long, cylindrical body, short legs, and a bushy tail. Different species have modifications that equip them for a certain lifestyle—climbing or gliding among the trees or burrowing underground. They are generally small animals; and the largest, the ground-dwelling European marmot, is no more than 29 inches (74 cm) long and weighs less than 18 pounds (8 kg). Tree squirrels are much more slightly built than ground squirrels. The biggest, the Indian giant squirrel, can be up to 35 inches (90 cm), but two-thirds of its length is its tail. Even large specimens weigh no more than 7 pounds (3 kg). The smallest squirrel is the African pygmy squirrel. At less than 4 inches (10 cm) long, it can weigh as little as a third of an ounce (10 g).

The hind feet have five long toes in most species (four in the woodchuck). The soles and palms have pads of thickened skin that help improve grip. Squirrels have dexterous front paws with four longish fingers and a small thumb. They often sit up and use their hands to hold and manipulate food, a characteristic and appealing behavior. Teamed with their alert manner, bright eyes, and twitchy nose, squirrels are charming animals to watch, and their daytime habits make them relatively easy to observe. However, squirrels are not always popular. They make themselves a nuisance by "stealing" from bird feeders or raiding fruit, nut, and vegetable crops. Burrowing species can also create a hazard to livestock and farm machinery.

Squirrels have many enemies, and being active in the day makes them potential prey for many predatory mammals and birds. But the positioning of the eyes on the side of the head gives a wide field of vision, and squirrels have sharp hearing, so they are not easy to approach undetected. Their best defense is their lifestyle and behavior: When danger threatens, most species can either escape to the trees or disappear underground.

Family Sciuridae: 2 subfamilies, 50 genera, about 270 species

Subfamily Sciurinae (tree, ground, rock, bush, dwarf, sun, and giant squirrels, prairie dogs, marmots, and chipmunks) 36 genera, about 230 species including:

Cynomys, such as black-tailed prairie dog (*C. ludovicianus*)

Ratufa, such as Indian giant squirrel (*R. indica*)

Marmota, such as European marmot (*M. marmota*); woodchuck (*M. monax*)

Myosciurus, such as African pygmy squirrel (*M. pumilio*)

Sciurus, such as Eurasian red squirrel (*S. vulgaris*); gray squirrel (*S. carolinensis*); eastern fox squirrel (*S. niger*)

Spermophilus, such as thirteen-lined ground squirrel (*S. tridecemlineatus*)

Tamias, such as eastern chipmunk (*T. striatus*)

Funambulus, such as northern striped palm squirrel (*F. pennantii*)

Subfamily Petauristinae (flying squirrels) 14 genera, 40 species including:

Aeromys, such as black flying squirrel (*A. tephromelas*)

Glaucomys, such as southern flying squirrel (*G. volans*)

Hylopetes, such as red-cheeked flying squirrel (*H. spadiceus*)

Petinomys, such as Mindanao flying squirrel (*P. crinitus*)

---

34   **SEE ALSO** Squirrel, Gray **7**:38; Squirrel, Eurasian Red **7**:42; Woodchuck **7**:50; Squirrel, Indian Giant **7**:62

Seasonal Survival

Squirrels occur naturally on every continent apart from Antarctica and Australasia. They are found in most terrestrial habitats except hot, dry deserts such as the Sahara Desert in Africa and the Atacama Desert in South America. In the tropics, where food of some kind is available all year round, squirrels remain active and switch between foods as different plants come into season. Most squirrels living in temperate zones are less active in winter, when food is harder to find and bad weather makes looking for it difficult and dangerous. There are two ways of dealing with the problem: Either shut down completely and hibernate, relying on reserves of body fat to survive; or store away enough food during summer to supplement otherwise meager winter rations and remain active throughout the year. Tree squirrels, which eat nuts and seeds tend to opt for the latter strategy, since their food is abundant in the fall and can easily be collected and stored. Nuts keep well and are packed with fat and protein. Also, tree squirrels cannot become excessively fat

The northern striped palm squirrel is found in parts of India, Nepal, and Pakistan. The species is quite social, and several animals can often be observed in the same tree.

without compromising their agility. Marmots, on the other hand, eat mainly green shoots and vegetation and would have to store a massive volume of hay to see them through. Instead, they rely on fat stored within their own body. They fall into a deep sleep, allowing their core temperature and metabolic rate to slow down dramatically so that no energy is wasted and use their fat to keep their body going over winter.

Climbers and Burrowers

Climbing trees and digging burrows may seem like very different ways of making a living, but in fact both options offer squirrels the same important benefit—fewer large predators than at ground level. Adaptations to climbing include a relatively slim, lightweight body, strong, curved claws, and well-developed finger, arm, and abdominal

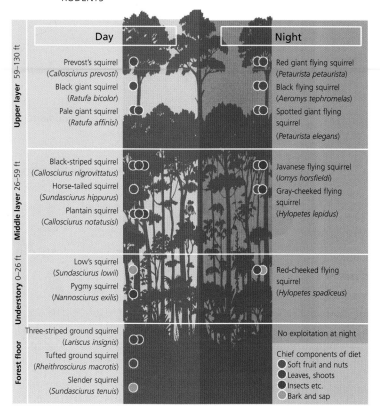

	Day	Night
Upper layer 59–130 ft	Prevost's squirrel (*Callosciurus prevosti*) Black giant squirrel (*Ratufa bicolor*) Pale giant squirrel (*Ratufa affinisi*)	Red giant flying squirrel (*Petaurista petaurista*) Black flying squirrel (*Aeromys tephromelas*) Spotted giant flying squirrel (*Petaurista elegans*)
Middle layer 26–59 ft	Black-striped squirrel (*Callosciurus nigrovittatus*) Horse-tailed squirrel (*Sundasciurus hippurus*) Plantain squirrel (*Callosciurus notatusisi*)	Javanese flying squirrel (*Iomys horsfieldi*) Gray-cheeked flying squirrel (*Hylopetes lepidus*)
Understory 0–26 ft	Low's squirrel (*Sundasciurus lowii*) Pygmy squirrel (*Nannosciurus exilis*)	Red-cheeked flying squirrel (*Hylopetes spadiceus*)
Forest floor	Three-striped ground squirrel (*Lariscus insignis*) Tufted ground squirrel (*Rheithrosciurus macrotis*) Slender squirrel (*Sundasciurus tenuis*)	No exploitation at night Chief components of diet ● Soft fruit and nuts ● Leaves, shoots ● Insects etc. ● Bark and sap

⤊ *For two or more species to live in the same habitat, they must exploit different food resources. The diagram above illustrates how species of squirrel living in the lowland forests of Malaysia survive harmoniously.*

muscles. Eyes at the side of the head are good for judging distance. Tree squirrels have extremely flexible ankle joints that can rotate 180 degrees so that the squirrel can run down trees headfirst. When doing so, its hind feet point back up the tree, with its sharp claws hooking into the bark to prevent the squirrel falling. Tree-climbing animals that lack this useful adaptation, such as martens, are forced to descend backward in a series of ungainly jumps. The advantages for the squirrels are obvious—not only can they climb down very quickly, but they can also see where they are going! Tree squirrels have much longer tails than ground dwellers. The tail is used as counterbalance, flicking from side to side, and enabling the squirrel to run along narrow branches and even telephone wires.

Ground squirrels are usually recognizable by their more robustly built body. The forelegs are more muscular than in tree squirrels, with strong, blunt claws more suited to scraping soil than gripping. The tail is generally not bushy and quite short.

Sexual and Social Organization

The social and mating systems of squirrels are very diverse. In hibernating species the breeding season is compressed, and adults begin looking for mates almost as soon as they wake in the spring—in the case of some marmots, before they even emerge from their snowed-in burrows. Many species are territorial. Males of most ground squirrel species defend large territories, each overlapping the home ranges of several females with whom they claim exclusive breeding rights. In other species females have more say in the matter. Female gray squirrels, among others, encourage males to chase them through the treetops. The chase may begin with just one or two suitors, but soon attracts the attention of others. Before long there may be as many as 10 males in hot pursuit. The chase allows the female to see which male is strongest and fastest in order to help her choose the best father for her offspring.

Squirrels and the Landscape

The activities of squirrels can have a profound effect on the environment in which they live. For example, prairie dogs (colonial ground squirrels) create huge communal burrow systems. These "towns" once covered vast areas of land in the North American Midwest. Prairie dogs do not like tall vegetation that might conceal predators, so they cut it down with their teeth. After a time their constant nibbling means that only low-growing plants survive, and the whole nature of the prairie ecosystem begins to change into a more open environment.

⊕ *"Flying" squirrels have developed the ability to glide between the trees in an effort to avoid predators on the ground.*

Foresters traditionally dislike squirrels because they can damage trees. Debarking is an especially damaging habit by which tree squirrels strip off bark to get to the soft, sappy tissues underneath. That can allow infection by fungal disease and may even kill the tree if the trunk is debarked all the way around—known as "ringing." However, many squirrels, particularly nonhibernating species that cache food for winter, also play a beneficial role in woodland ecology. Food stores are made by burying nuts and acorns, usually one at a time, in the soil or leaf litter some distance from the tree that produced them. The squirrel remembers the location of the storage area rather than the precise location of individual nuts, so inevitably some are never recovered and stand a chance of germinating at a later date. That is how many trees get their seeds distributed. Whenever a tree falls in the forest, new seedlings are ready to fill the gap. Trees that produced the squirrel's food benefit by having seeds widely scattered and already planted, just waiting for the touch of the sun to awaken them.

Taking to the Air

Among the mammals only bats are capable of true powered flight, but the flying squirrels, colugos, and marsupial gliding possums have achieved a limited mastery of the air by evolving the ability to glide.

Traveling by air is a bold solution to the problem faced by many small arboreal mammals: how to cross safely from tree to tree. Coming down to ground level exposes the squirrels to all kinds of predators—cats, wolves, weasels, and large lizards to name but a few. In the trees the squirrels are still vulnerable to birds of prey, but most can be avoided by the squirrels' habit of being nocturnal. The main predators of flying squirrels are owls. However, the rodents have strategies for minimizing that risk too. The moment they land on a tree, they immediately scurry around to the other side. They then dash upward so that an owl in hot pursuit suddenly finds several inches of solid trunk between it and its intended prey.

⊕ *Cape, or South African, ground squirrels sun themselves in the Kalahari Gemsbok National Park. The species lives in colonies averaging five to 10 members, but can number as many as 25 to 30 individuals.*

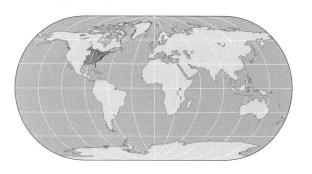

Common name Gray squirrel
(American gray squirrel)

Scientific name *Sciurus carolinensis*

Family	Sciuridae
Order	Rodentia
Size	Length head/body: 9–11 in (24–29 cm); tail length: 8–9 in (20–24 cm)

Weight 14–21 oz (400–600 g)

Key features Chunky squirrel with variable silvery to dark-gray fur, tinged with brown in summer; black individuals or subgroups also occur; tail bushy and fringed with white; ears rounded and without hairy tips

Habits	Diurnal; tree-dwelling; also forages extensively on the ground; solitary, but nonterritorial; bold and inquisitive
Breeding	One or 2 litters of 1–7 young born January–February and May–June after gestation period of 44–45 days. Weaned at 8 weeks; females sexually mature at 8 months, males at 10–11 months. May live up to 10 years in captivity, usually fewer in the wild
Voice	Churring and chattering sounds; screams in distress
Diet	Seeds and nuts, especially acorns; also buds, flowers, fruit, insects, and eggs
Habitat	Mixed deciduous woodland
Distribution	Southeastern Canada and eastern U.S.; introduced populations in Britain, Italy, and South Africa
Status	Population: abundant

Gray Squirrel

Sciurus carolinensis

The gray squirrel is a native of North America, but thanks to widespread introductions it is now a familiar animal in parts of Europe too.

WITH ITS BRIGHT EYES, GREAT AGILITY, and inquisitive nature the gray squirrel is an appealing animal. It is also adaptable and can make the most of a wide variety of habitats. Its needs are simple: food and trees that are out of reach of predators in which to rear young. Its flexibility, along with a certain hardiness and tolerance of cold winter weather, has made the animal a big success in its native North America. Elsewhere, it thrives as a not altogether welcome alien.

Tree Houses

Gray squirrels will take advantage of holes in trees or hollow branches in which to build secure nests, where they shelter from the elements and raise their young. However, such ready-made nest sites are not very abundant, and in the absence of a tree hole most squirrels opt for self-built accommodation. Squirrels' nests (known as dreys) are highly distinctive. Slightly larger than a soccer ball, they are built of skillfully interwoven twigs nibbled from the same tree. Summer nests are built high in the tree tops, usually in a convenient fork and hidden from view by leafy branches. Winter dreys need to be a bit more robust in order to withstand buffeting winds and other winter weather. Dreys built in deciduous trees are inevitably rather exposed in winter, so the squirrels generally build close to the trunk where there is some shelter from the wind and rain and less movement in high winds.

Gray squirrels forage both in trees and on the ground. In natural habitats they feed mostly on nuts, pine cones, other seeds, and bark, but

⊕ *A female American gray snacks in Stanley Park, Vancouver. Squirrels are a common sight in parks and gardens across North America and Europe. Black phases like this one are often seen in the north of their range.*

The Bird-Feeder Challenge

For some people the gray squirrel's intelligence and its bold, inquisitive nature are part of its charm. For others the same characteristics result in a long-running battle of wits that more often than not the squirrels win. Garden bird-feeders provide an exceptionally good food source for any animal or bird that can reach them. Fat- and energy-rich foods such as nuts, seeds, and kitchen scraps are ample reward for a few hours spent solving the problem of access. The squirrels' ingenuity sometimes appears to know no bounds as time and again they figure out how to reach feeders hung in tricky places. Gray squirrels can climb bird tables and negotiate large overhangs with ease. They can run nimbly along wires and washing lines, haul up peanut feeders hung on string, bring down those suspended by wire, or split them open from the sides, spilling the nuts onto the ground. Some people gain a good deal of pleasure from devising new challenges for their garden squirrels, then sitting back and watching these smart rodents complete increasingly complicated obstacle courses for the reward of a handful of nuts.

The reward makes all the effort worthwhile—a squirrel negotiates a garden bird feeder.

they are happy to take food left out for birds and will regularly raid trashcans and unattended picnics. In parks and gardens they frequently become tame enough to take food from human hands. Like other squirrels, they sit up to feed and use their dexterous front paws to manipulate food. They lack a thumb, so they use two paws for grasping objects securely.

⬆ *A squirrel builds a nest in a hollow tree. Tree hollows are prime nesting sites for gray squirrels, providing shelter from the elements and a secure place to raise young.*

Most of the gray squirrel's natural food is seasonal, with late summer and fall being boom times. Squirrels take full advantage of the glut of nuts and acorns, and their appetite for mast is one of the main reasons for the massive overproduction of seeds by some trees. A single tree only has to produce one successful seed to reproduce itself, and yet the average oak produces thousands of acorns every year for centuries. In fact, millions of years of coexistence has resulted in mast trees and mast-eating animals (such as squirrels) adopting mutually beneficial strategies that help ensure their survival. A large tree produces huge crops of nuts, attracting squirrels to feed. But because the glut only lasts for a few weeks, the squirrels have learned to store excess nuts for the leaner times ahead. The gray squirrel buries nuts among the leaf litter and loose soil of the forest floor. It buries so many in a certain area that it does not need to remember the precise location of each nut. When the squirrel returns, all it has to do is dig and it will find food. Inevitably, some of the hidden nuts are never recovered, and they lie dormant in the soil, awaiting the chance to germinate.

Solitary Lives

Most female gray squirrels produce litters in spring and summer. The young squirrels spend their early lives in a secure nest, emerging at about six weeks old to begin exploring the treetops. Once they have left their mother's care, they are not especially sociable, although adults of both sexes will share nests in very cold weather. But for most of the year relationships are not quite so friendly. Males are especially pugnacious in the presence of an estrous female, and fights between rival suitors can result in bites, torn ears, and chunks of missing fur. Annoyance or aggression is signaled with growls and tail-wagging displays.

In their native North America gray and other tree squirrels are still common animals, although apparently less so than in the past. Their decline is due in part to man-made changes in their habitat and in particular to the

⬇ *A gray squirrel strips the bark from a sycamore tree in the hope of uncovering sappy tissue on which to feed. But its action can kill the tree.*

widespread loss of the American chestnut tree. In the 19th century squirrel populations could reach almost plague proportions during the summer and fall, when chestnuts were plentiful. If a hard winter followed, hordes of squirrels would perform mass migrations in search of more productive habitats. In the late 1960s millions of squirrels were killed every year, in part for their fur. The silvery coat of the gray squirrel is soft and warm, and was once fashionable. Squirrel hunting is now more closely regulated throughout most of the United States. Across the Atlantic in Britain the gray squirrel is doing so well that its total eradication, deemed by some to be desirable, seems virtually impossible.

Costly Imports

The gray squirrel's conquest of Britain began in the late 19th century, when the first animals were imported from the United States. The intention was to "improve" Britain's existing wildlife by adding new species to the fauna. This was in spite of the fact that Britain already had its own successful native squirrel—the highly arboreal red squirrel. However, gray squirrels are undeniably attractive animals with appealing behavioral characteristics and are easy to catch and transport.

The first batch of gray squirrels was released in England in 1876, and many more followed over the next 50 years. The species did exceptionally well; and by 1930, when the less desirable consequences of their spread were realized, it was too late to reverse the trend. As the gray population boomed, the red squirrel entered a dramatic decline. Despite vigorous attempts to control their number, gray squirrels thrived, and by 1960 they had colonized all but the far north of England and Scotland. As the gray squirrel spread, the native species was displaced and steadily died out over large areas. Gray squirrels have caused similar problems in Ireland and have now been released in northern Italy. They have also been taken to South Africa, where they are responsible for significant damage to native and plantation trees.

Common name Eurasian red squirrel

Scientific name *Sciurus vulgaris*

Family   Sciuridae

Order   Rodentia

Size   Length head/body: 7–9.5 in (18–24 cm); tail length: 5.5–8 in (14–20 cm)

Weight 7–17 oz (200–480 g)

Key features Dainty squirrel with rich reddish-brown fur, white chest, and bushy tail; ears have long tufts in winter

Habits   Active by day; arboreal; very agile; generally solitary; does not hibernate

Breeding   One or 2 litters of 1–8 (usually 3) young born in spring or summer after gestation period of 6 weeks. Weaned at 7–10 weeks; sexually mature at 10–12 months. May live 10 years in captivity, up to 7 in the wild

Voice   Chattering and chucking sounds

Diet   Pine cones, nuts, acorns, fruit, bark, and sap

Habitat   Woodland, especially conifer

Distribution Most of Europe except southern England and northern and eastern Italy, where introduced gray squirrel thrives; Asia east to northeastern China

Status   Population: abundant; IUCN Lower Risk: near threatened. Locally threatened in areas where gray squirrels have been introduced

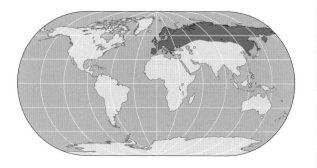

Eurasian Red Squirrel

Sciurus vulgaris

The Eurasian red squirrel is a typical tree squirrel. It can move quickly and nimbly on the ground, but it is much more at home in the treetops, where it moves with astounding speed and agility.

THE EURASIAN RED SQUIRREL is a different species than the American red squirrel, and both are considerably smaller than the gray squirrel. Its lightweight body allows it to venture to the very tips of slender branches, and it can move from tree to tree with spectacular leaps. Its agility is never better demonstrated than during the long mating chases that occur in spring and summer.

A Merry Dance

The mating chases are initiated by females and can involve as many as five males in pursuit. The female sprints through trees, twisting and leaping and appearing to try her hardest to escape her admirers. She only allows herself to be "caught" when she has had a chance to size up the options—she wants the best male to father her offspring. Once she has accepted a male, he will mate with her and spend some time guarding her from his rivals. However, his interest is short-lived, and he will be long gone by the time her babies arrive.

Red squirrels are not normally territorial, but in spring the males will compete for status, and aggressive encounters can be common. In the fall each squirrel begins to bury nuts in the ground ready for winter. The caches are yet another source of tension, with squirrels using angry chattering sounds to warn off intruders. Squirrels of all ages, even juveniles, hoard nuts and seeds. Poaching by other squirrels is not uncommon, and some individuals will scatter

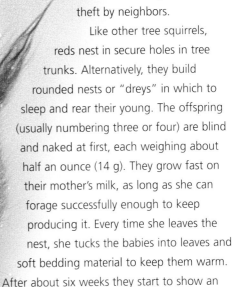

their stores widely to avoid theft by neighbors.

Like other tree squirrels, reds nest in secure holes in tree trunks. Alternatively, they build rounded nests or "dreys" in which to sleep and rear their young. The offspring (usually numbering three or four) are blind and naked at first, each weighing about half an ounce (14 g). They grow fast on their mother's milk, as long as she can forage successfully enough to keep producing it. Every time she leaves the nest, she tucks the babies into leaves and soft bedding material to keep them warm. After about six weeks they start to show an interest in the outside world, and by eight weeks they are weaned and have to begin finding their own food. Many young squirrels die at this stage, but those that survive quickly increase their skill and confidence in the trees.

Reds and Grays

The red squirrel is best suited to life in coniferous woodland, but throughout much of its range it also occupies mixed and deciduous forests. It feeds on nuts, fruit, sap, and especially pine cones. It strips the seeds from the cones with its sharp incisors and tosses away the empty cone like the core of an apple. Fresh, ripe nuts are levered open, shattering the shell into pieces. One food the red squirrel does not eat is acorns. Unlike American gray squirrels, reds are unable to digest the toxins in acorns, and eating them may make red squirrels ill. Hence in a deciduous woodland with plenty of oak trees gray squirrels can live at approximately double the density of reds. In the natural scheme of things that should not be a problem, since Eurasian red and American gray squirrels live on different continents. However, in Britain, Ireland, and Italy introductions of gray squirrels in the last 100 years have caused a serious challenge to the red squirrel, which is now in decline as a result of competition from its more adaptable American cousin.

⊝ The red squirrel of Europe and Central Asia has distinctive tufting on its ears in winter. In Russia it is hunted for its dark-brown winter coat.

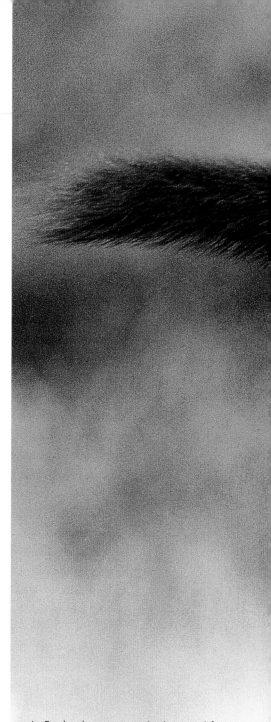

Gray squirrels do not kill reds, even though they are larger and potentially aggressive. Nor do they carry a disease that wipes out red squirrels (although they are more resistant to the *parapox* virus, which occurs naturally in squirrels). Grays are simply better adapted to life in temperate mixed woodland. Their larger bodies mean they can put on more fat and survive better in harsh winters. They forage more on the ground than red squirrels and so have a greater range of foods to rely on, especially when nut crops fail. Red squirrels cannot make use of acorns, the commonest form of nuts in many European woodlands, but grays thrive on them. In the absence of gray squirrels reds can get by; but once a population of grays expands, the reds are edged out.

A Tale of a Tail

According to the popular story by Victorian children's author Beatrix Potter, Squirrel Nutkin was a very naughty red squirrel who delighted in tormenting Old Brown Owl with silly riddles when he should have been gathering hazelnuts. Eventually, Old Brown catches him and tries to skin him alive, but Nutkin escapes by leaving his tail behind. According to the story, Nutkin now waits in the trees and heckles passers by, especially those who ask him riddles!

The loss of his tail was a serious punishment for Squirrel Nutkin. Without its tail a red squirrel's agility would be seriously impaired because it no longer has anything with which to balance its body weight—a bit like a tightrope walker without a pole. The tail has other uses too, such as signaling from a distance. A fiercely wagging tail is a sure sign of hostility and is often the prelude to a fight. Being extremely bushy, the red squirrel's tail also serves as a blanket in winter—squirrels sleep with their tail wrapped around them for extra warmth. Furthermore, as a male squirrel, poor Nutkin would find that his missing tail makes him far less attractive to females, even if he were able to catch one in the frenzy of a mating chase.

Illustration from **The Tale of Squirrel Nutkin** *by* **Beatrix Potter.**

In England, as gray squirrels spread from their original release points during the early 20th century, reds typically disappeared within 15 years. The species is now extinct in southern England except for on a few islands that grays have not yet reached. In the north and in Scotland the reds only hold their own in coniferous woodland, where they are more at home than grays. Grays can eat pine cones, but they are too heavy-bodied to collect them from the tips of narrow branches, so the reds have an advantage here. Where there are no acorns to supplement their diet, often the case in northern areas, grays are at a disadvantage.

Limited Conservation Success

The options for conserving the red squirrel in Europe are limited. Reintroducing red squirrels to places from which they have disappeared is pointless if gray squirrels are still around. Also, the reds are highly strung animals, and the stress of being captured and moved would result in many deaths. Several attempts at translocating red squirrels have already failed.

Another possibility would be to try to eradicate the introduced grays. However, that would be a huge operation, and public opposition to killing millions of undeniably cute animals is strong. A third option is to try to balance out the unequal competition between the two species by providing the red squirrels with extra food. Fairer distribution of food could be achieved by using special food dispensers that can only be reached by the smaller, lighter red squirrels. Most such devices have some kind of trapdoor that swings open if a heavy gray squirrel enters, dumping it unceremoniously on the ground below. However, conservation of this type would have to continue indefinitely, and so far there is no evidence that it helps very much. As long as there are gray squirrels in Europe, the red squirrel will continue to be threatened.

↑ *The Eurasian red squirrel is capable of spectacular leaps. Leaping is a behavior seen particularly in the spring and summer, when males pursue females through the trees in mating chases.*

Common name Eastern fox squirrel

Scientific name *Sciurus niger*

Family Sciuridae

Order Rodentia

Size Length head/body: 17.5–27.5 in (45–70 cm); tail length: 8–10 in (20–30 cm)

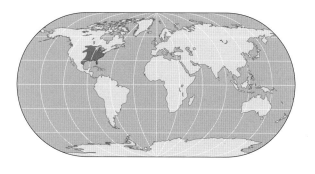

Weight 1.1–2.2 lb (0.5–0.9 kg)

Key features Larger than other tree squirrels; coat a variable shade of gold, rusty red, or black; feet cinnamon colored, tail almost black

Habits Diurnal; tree-dwelling; solitary

Breeding One or 2 litters of 1–7 young born January–February and May–June after gestation period of 44–45 days. Weaned at 8 weeks; females sexually mature at 8 months, males at 10–11 months. May live up to 18 years in captivity, 8 in the wild

Voice Sharp barks, chattering, and whining sounds; screams in distress

Diet Seeds and nuts, especially acorns; also fruit, insects, and eggs

Habitat Mixed deciduous woodland

Distribution Central and eastern U.S. as far south as northeastern Mexico; introduced to some western states

Status Population: abundant. Hunted as game under seasonal regulation

Eastern Fox Squirrel

Sciurus niger

The eastern fox squirrel is the largest member of the genus Sciurus, *but is otherwise a typical member of the specialized tree-dwelling group of rodents.*

THE NATURAL RANGE OF THE eastern fox squirrel includes most of the eastern and central United States. It has been successfully introduced to some western states, including California, Oregon, and Colorado. It has always been a familiar animal in the countryside, city parks, and gardens of eastern states, but is now also common in San Francisco and Seattle. The scientific name *niger* means "black," but fox squirrels from different parts of the species' huge range differ significantly in terms of coat color. In the north they are typically gray with a yellowish belly, in the west the fur has a reddish tinge, and in the south they are often black with a white-tipped tail, facial stripe, and sometimes white ear tips, too.

Soccer-Ball Nests

Fox squirrels are strictly diurnal and most active in the morning and late afternoon. They will often take a siesta in one of several nests scattered around the home range. Nests may be built in hollow trees or constructed from scratch using branches and twigs severed from the tree by the squirrel's sharp teeth. Such nests are roughly the size and shape of a soccer ball and quite easy to spot in winter when the trees lose their leaves. In midwinter the normal routine changes slightly. Shorter days mean that there is less time for foraging, and the squirrel may have to use every available hour of daylight in order to find enough food. The eastern fox squirrel does not hibernate, although it may be temporarily confined to its nest by strong winds, rain, or exceptionally cold weather.

The fox squirrel shares parts of its range with the American gray squirrel, but avoids direct competition by feeding at slightly different times of day and spending more time foraging on the ground. Its preferred foods are nuts and acorns from hickory, walnut, and oak trees. It also feeds on fruit—especially mulberries. Nuts are levered open with the lower incisors, splitting the shell into fragments before removing the kernel. Nuts can be eaten even when small and green. The squirrels often get a bad name by raiding nut orchards before the crop has had a chance to ripen.

Male and female fox squirrels occupy different home ranges at different times of year, moving around as seasonal food sources come and go. In the course of a year the average squirrel uses a range of about 40 acres (16 ha). Young animals dispersing from their mother's range travel even farther. Male fox squirrels disperse farther than females and are more vulnerable to predation, so the sex ratio in most populations is biased in favor of females. Fox squirrels are not territorial, but they tend to avoid each other's company and will protest loudly if another squirrel comes too close, making chattering sounds and waving their tails in annoyance.

High-Speed Chase

During the breeding season males congregate in the range of an estrous female and compete for dominance. Every male that thinks he has a chance joins in a high-speed mating chase. The winner usually gets to mate with the female and then spends some time trying to guard her from his rivals. However, he soon loses interest in his prize and plays no part in the raising of his offspring. Experienced mothers are known to breed early in the year and often have time to fit in a second litter in the summer. First-time mothers, on the other hand, usually start to breed in their second year and manage just one litter.

⊖ *The eastern fox squirrel is a common sight in urban parks and gardens of the eastern United States, being active mostly in the morning and late afternoon.*

Common name Eastern chipmunk

Scientific name *Tamias striatus*

Family Sciuridae

Order Rodentia

Size Length head/body: 5.5–7 in (14–17 cm); tail length: 3–5 in (8–12 cm)

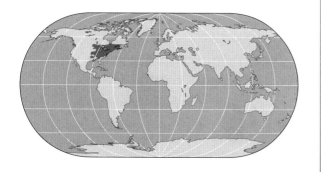

Weight 3–5 oz (85–140 g)

Key features Large chipmunk with reddish-brown coat, fading to cream on belly, with 5 black stripes along back separated alternately by brown-and-white fur; large internal cheek pouches; bottlebrush tail covered in short hair; ears rounded, eyes large and bright; face also has striped markings

Habits Diurnal; solitary; territorial; digs extensive burrows—may stay there in winter, but does not hibernate

Breeding One or 2 litters of 1–9 (usually 3–5) young born in spring and summer after gestation period of 31 days. Weaned at 6 weeks; sexually mature at 10–12 months. May live up to 8 years in captivity, 3 in the wild

Voice High-pitched chirping calls

Diet Nuts, seeds, acorns, fungi, fruit, and crop plants; occasionally insects, birds' eggs, and baby mice

Habitat Lightly wooded land with warm, dry soils and rocky crevices in which to hide

Distribution Eastern U.S. and southeastern Canada

Status Population: abundant. Threatened by persecution and habitat loss in some agricultural areas

Eastern Chipmunk

Tamias striatus

The eastern chipmunk is one of the most widespread and best known members of the genus Tamias. *Its name means "treasurer"—a reference to the chipmunk's compulsive hoarding of nuts and seeds to help see it through the winter months.*

EASTERN CHIPMUNKS ARE LARGER than the other 24 species of *Tamias* and are generally found in areas of relatively light deciduous woodland. They are especially fond of places with broken rocky ground or old stone walls, since they provide plenty of secure nooks and crannies in which to hide from predators.

Excavation Skills

Chipmunks of this species are accomplished diggers, and their burrows can extend up to 30 feet (9 m) underground. The entrance to the burrow is usually well hidden at the base of a rock or fallen log and often among a layer of loose leaves. Unlike some other ground-dwelling squirrels, the eastern chipmunk carries away soil excavated from its burrow for disposal so there is no telltale mound of spoil to give away its whereabouts. The soil is carried in two capacious cheek pouches, which open inside the chipmunk's mouth. The same pouches are also used for transporting food such as acorns and nuts. When full, the pouches are almost as large as the chipmunk's skull.

Stored food is a vital resource that enables chipmunks to survive the winter. Unlike their Siberian cousin *Tamias sibiricus*, American chipmunks do not enter full winter hibernation, and they need to continue feeding even when their homes are buried deep in snow. They therefore spend the fall gathering enough food

The eastern chipmunk has large cheek pouches in which to transport food items, as well as soil excavated from its burrow.

to see them through several months of enforced inactivity. They spend much of the winter asleep in their burrows, but wake regularly to feed and will emerge into the open during short periods of warmer weather. When spring finally arrives, they launch almost immediately into breeding activity and in good years manage to fit in two breeding seasons before the end of summer.

Belligerent Behavior

Adult eastern chipmunks are territorial and aggressive. The high-pitched "chip, chip, chip" call for which they are named is used to advertise boundaries and warn off intruders. Confrontations are common because, while core territories are small—usually no more than a 50-foot (15-m) radius around the burrow entrance—each chipmunk will regularly venture up to 150 feet (45 m) from its burrow to forage. While out and about it often meets with its neighbors.

Aggression reaches a peak during the mating season, when males gather in the territory of an estrous female to compete for her attention. However, the female still has the final word about which male fathers her offspring, and unworthy suitors are unceremoniously rejected. The young (usually numbering three to five) are born in the female's burrow and emerge into the open at about six weeks of age. At eight weeks they can fend for themselves and will disperse into the local area, usually settling nearby.

Many people enjoy watching chipmunks in parks and gardens throughout the animals' range. The chipmunks are bold, inquisitive, and charismatic and can be tamed fairly easily. However, despite their obvious appeal, they are also capable of causing serious damage to crops, garden plants, and other property. In some cases their burrows can destabilize fence posts and even undermine the foundations of buildings.

Common name Woodchuck
(groundhog,
whistlepig)

Scientific name *Marmota monax*

Family   Sciuridae

Order   Rodentia

Size   Length head/body: 16–26 in (41–66 cm); tail
               length: 4–10 in (10–25 cm)

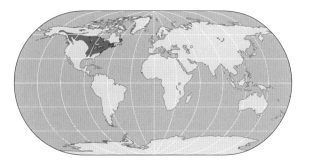

Weight 4.5–13 lb (2–6 kg)

Key features Chunky, short-legged,
short-tailed rodent; dense, woolly,
reddish-brown fur with white-tipped guard
hairs; head darker, with small eyes and small,
rounded ears; short, hairy tail

Habits   Diurnal; terrestrial; burrowing; hibernates in
               winter

Breeding   Single litter of 1–9 (usually 4 or 5) born in
               spring after gestation period of 30–32 days.
               Weaned at 6 weeks; sexually mature at 2
               years. May live up to 15 years in captivity,
               6 in the wild

Voice   Loud whistling alarm call; also makes
               chattering, squealing, and barking noises;
               grinds teeth when agitated

Diet   Fresh grasses and leaves of other plants; also
               seeds and fruit

Habitat   Prairie, grasslands, and road edges

Distribution North America: Alaska to Idaho in the west,
               Newfoundland to Alabama and Arkansas in
               the east

Status   Population: abundant. Has expanded range
               and population in some areas developed for
               agriculture, but hunting for fur and
               persecution as a pest have led to significant
               declines in others

Woodchuck *Marmota monax*

*Also known as the groundhog or whistlepig owing
to its high-pitched alarm call, the woodchuck is
one of North America's best-known rodents.*

THE AMERICAN WOODCHUCK is a species of
marmot—a kind of large, ground-dwelling,
burrowing squirrel. It is a highly proficient
digger: Its legs are short, powerful, and bear
strong claws to help loosen packed soil, which
is then shoved aside by the soles of the
woodchuck's flat feet.

Woodchuck burrows are extensive: Some
extend horizontally as much as 50 feet (15 m)
and have four or five entrances. The burrows
are a nuisance to farmers because they cause
damage to plowing machinery, undermine the
foundations of buildings, and pose a threat to
livestock, which can stumble into the holes. The
woodchuck tends to use different dens in
different seasons. In summer it lives and breeds
in burrows dug in open ground and marked by
a heap of fresh dirt at the entrance. In winter it
retreats to a less conspicuous burrow, usually
dug at the base of a tree. The roots may help
support the tunnel during wet weather.

Homeless Youngsters

In prime habitat woodchuck population
densities can exceed 37 per square mile
(15 per sq. km). Individual home ranges vary
with habitat and season. They can be as small
as half an acre (0.2 ha) for breeding females or
as large as 7.5 acres (3 ha) for males, whose
ranges usually overlap those of several females.
The woodchuck is the least social of the
marmots, and the ranges of males and females
tend not to overlap with those of other animals
of the same sex. Territories are advertised using
scent from three large glands under the tail,
and intruders are aggressively driven away.
Females can also be ruthless in expelling their
own offspring from their territory as soon as
they are able to fend for themselves—at about
six weeks old. Daughters are sometimes

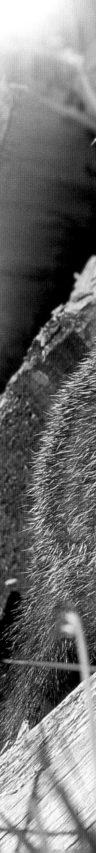

permitted to stay over the winter, but only if there is a good supply of food.

Unlike most other squirrels, woodchucks favor green leaves and shoots over energy-rich seed heads and nuts. Their relatively low fat and calorie content mean that woodchucks must eat a lot to sustain themselves, sometimes over 1 pound (0.4 kg) of vegetation every day. Their large appetites make woodchucks very unpopular with farmers—the hungry rodents can ruin crops such as alfalfa, corn, and oats.

Woodchucks must feed well in spring and summer because in winter they enter deep hibernation. The duration varies, but the animal usually emerges sometime in March or April. American folklore tells that if the woodchuck emerges on February 2 and sees its own shadow (i.e., if the sun is shining), there are six more weeks of wintry weather to come; if the day is cloudy, then spring is not far away. The precise origins of the story are obscure, but thanks to the 1993 movie of the same name millions of people have heard of "Groundhog Day" even if they do not know what it means!

⊕ *Two woodchucks in Minnesota perch on a plank of wood. The rodents are also known as groundhogs, and February 2 is "Groundhog Day."*

Common name European marmot (alpine marmot)

Scientific name *Marmota marmota*

Family Sciuridae

Order Rodentia

Size Length head/body: 18.5–20 in (47–52 cm); tail length: 6–8 in (15–20 cm)

Weight 6–10 lb (3–4.5 kg)

Key features Chunky body with short, muscular legs and short tail; fur is golden-brown to gray

Habits Diurnal; social; burrowing; hibernates for 6–7 months of the year

Breeding Single litter of 2–6 young born May–June after gestation period of 34 days. Weaned at 40 days; sexually mature at 18 months. May live up to 15 years in the wild, not often kept in captivity

Voice Shrill whistle when alarmed; growls and screeches when angry

Diet Grasses, herbs, roots, fruit, and flowers

Habitat Alpine meadows and rocky slopes above 1,970 ft (600 m)

Distribution Alpine regions of Italy, France, and Switzerland; reintroduced to Carpathian Mountains (Poland-Slovakia border); introduced to Germany (Black Forest) and France (Massif Central and Pyrenees, Vosges, and Jura Mountains)

Status Population: abundant. Has declined in recent centuries, but successfully reintroduced to areas of former (prehistoric) range

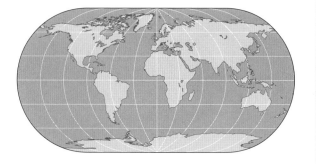

European Marmot

Marmota marmota

European marmots are large, heavily built ground squirrels. Their fat bodies and thick coats are adaptations to life at high altitudes. The word "marmot" is derived from the Latin murem montis, *meaning "mouse of the mountains."*

MARMOTS DO NOT COPE TOO WELL with heat. In midsummer their daytime activities are restricted to the morning and afternoon to avoid the midday sun. However, their dense fur and thick layer of body fat come into their own during the long alpine winters. At this time of year the marmots' preferred food of green shoots is scarce, and the animals are forced to hibernate in order to conserve energy. Hibernation occurs in a deep nest chamber within an extensive complex of burrows. The chamber is blocked with grass and dirt for winter security and to keep out damp and freezing drafts.

Stable Families

The European marmot lives in family groups with a joint home range of up to 11 acres (4.5 ha). It is one of the most social marmot species, since young animals need a prolonged period of parental care in order to survive the harsh climate. The nucleus of the family is a mated pair, and the unit also contains the offspring of the past two or three summers. Only the dominant female may breed, usually with the dominant male, but sometimes she will mate with one of her sons or with a wandering male from another family. Young animals stay with the family group for at least two years, but usually three. The dominant male keeps watch over his family's territory and will forcibly eject unrelated males. Like lions, occasionally, a new male will overthrow an elderly or unfit male, kill any young of the year, and take over the colony.

Marmots are equipped with excellent sight and hearing. They also have a good sense of

smell, and they use saliva secreted from their cheek glands to scent mark their territory. Group bonds are cemented by frequent close physical contact, including nuzzling and mutual grooming. Several vocalizations are used in communication, the most common being a warning call in the form of a shrill whistle. The call is sometimes repeated a number of times.

Both parents play a part in caring for the young. The mother suckles her babies, and the dominant male and other members of the family keep an eye on them when they are outside the burrow. During hibernation adult and subadult marmots will snuggle close to their younger brothers and sisters in the burrow in order to keep them from freezing. Although the body temperature cools to save energy, it remains considerably warmer than the air temperature, which sinks well below freezing. Sharing body warmth undoubtedly boosts the youngsters' chances of survival; but even so, winter mortality is high in marmots of all ages, and one in five will not survive.

Childless Years

If the dominant breeding female has used too much of her fat reserves over the winter, she may fail to breed. In other animal societies a healthier subordinate female would normally take over, but that does not happen with the European marmot. Instead, the absence of offspring gives the entire colony a chance to fatten up without the burden of caring for youngsters. By the following spring every member will be in prime condition and ready to make a success of breeding once again.

⊕ *Two European marmots investigate potential food by sniffing. Sense of smell in the species is well enough developed to recognize the scent of individual animals.*

Common name Thirteen-lined ground squirrel (thirteen-lined suslik)

Scientific name *Spermophilus tridecemlineatus* (*Citellus tridecemlineatus*)

Family Sciuridae

Order Rodentia

Size Length head/body: 4–7 in (11–18 cm); tail length: 2.5–5 in (6–13 cm)

Weight 4–5 oz (110–140 g). Weight can almost double prior to hibernation

Key features Compact body with short legs and furry tail up to about half length of body; coat strikingly marked with 13 alternating dark and pale stripes; the dark stripes are patterned with white spots

Habits Diurnal; burrowing; hibernates for up to 8 months a year

Breeding One (occasionally 2) litters of 2–13 young born in summer after gestation period of 28 days. Weaned at 6 weeks; sexually mature at 9–10 months. Females may live up to 11 years in captivity, similar in the wild; males about half as long

Voice Twittering chirps and chattering sounds; growls and piercing whistle used as alarm call

Diet Grasses and other herbs; seeds, insects (especially beetles, grasshoppers, and caterpillars); also eggs, baby mice, and birds

Habitat Grass prairie and farmland

Distribution Southern Canada (Alberta) south to Ohio and southern Texas

Status Population: abundant

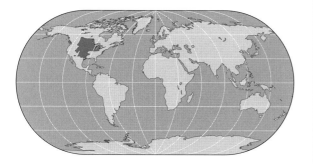

Thirteen-Lined Ground Squirrel

Spermophilus tridecemlineatus

The boldly patterned thirteen-lined ground squirrel is one of about three dozen American and Eurasian species belonging to the genus Spermophilus, *which literally translated means "seed-lover."*

THE GROUND SQUIRRELS' FONDNESS for seeds and grains makes many species unpopular with farmers. The thirteen-lined ground squirrel redeems itself somewhat by also eating large quantities of insects such as beetles and grasshoppers, which can themselves be serious agricultural pests. Unlike some species of *Spermophilus*, which have declined as their habitat has been taken over by humans, the thirteen-lined species thrives in areas where its natural prairie habitat is modified to grow crops. It also favors areas where forests are felled to make way for agriculture.

Strikingly Marked

The classification of the ground squirrels is tricky because many species appear similar. However, there is no mistaking the thirteen-lined ground squirrel, which is much more strikingly marked than its close relatives. From the age of about three weeks individual squirrels are marked with 13 bold black and buffy-white stripes down the back. The black stripes are further adorned with white spots, making the thirteen-lined ground squirrel one of the world's most decorative and attractive rodent species.

Thirteen-lined ground squirrels are active by day, but only during the summer months. In the fall, when food becomes scarce, they enter a long hibernation of up to 240 days. They sleep in grass-lined chambers excavated at the end of tunnels 16 to 20 feet (5 to 6 m) in length. The same tunnels are used for shelter during the

the four or five months it is active as fat is laid down for winter. Individuals also collect seeds in their cheek pouches and cache them away underground so that they are guaranteed a good breakfast when they wake up, even if spring is late coming and food still scarce.

Race Against Time

With such short periods of activity each year it is vital that breeding efforts start as soon as possible after the squirrels emerge from their winter sleep. Males begin seeking mates about two weeks after waking, and the first litters are born four weeks later. Experienced females tend to have large families of up to 12 young, while first-time mothers bear smaller litters of three or four. There is hardly time for the offspring to wean and fatten up before they need to enter hibernation. Late summer sees a race against time for youngsters trying to build up reserves to survive the winter. When to stop feeding and enter hibernation is a difficult judgment. Every day that the squirrel is active costs it more in terms of energy. Yet if it is underweight, it must continue foraging for foods that get harder to find as winter approaches.

⊕ *The thirteen-lined ground squirrel is small and easily hidden among grass, where its patterned coat breaks up its outline.*

active season and for rearing young. The entrances are usually concealed at the base of rocks or fence posts, and ground squirrel communities are often strung out along the fence lines that cross open farmland. Unlike many other species of *Spermophilus*, they are neither particularly social nor territorial, although each adult likes to keep a burrow for its own personal use.

Hibernation removes the need to eat during winter, since the sleeping animals live off reserves of fat accumulated during the summer: A healthy adult doubles its body weight during

Common name Black-tailed
prairie dog (plains prairie dog)

Scientific name *Cynomys ludovicianus*

Family   Sciuridae

Order   Rodentia

Size   Length head/body: 10–12 in (26–31 cm); tail
length: 3–4 in (7–9.5 cm). Female about 10%
smaller than male

Weight 20–53 oz (575–1,500 g)

Key features Sturdily built squirrel with short legs and
short tail with black tip; coat buffy gray

Habits   Diurnal and fossorial; highly social but also
territorial; does not hibernate

Breeding   Single litter of 1–8 (usually 3–5) young born
in spring after gestation period of 34–37
days. Weaned at 5–7 weeks; sexually mature
at 2 years. May live up to 8 years in captivity,
5 in the wild

Voice   Various barks, squeaks, and soft churring
sounds

Diet   Grasses and herbs

Habitat   Open short-grass plains and prairies; also
pastureland

Distribution Great Plains of North America from
southern Canada (Saskatchewan) to northern
Mexico

Status   Population: more than 1 million; IUCN Lower
Risk: near threatened. Has declined due to
habitat modification and persecution

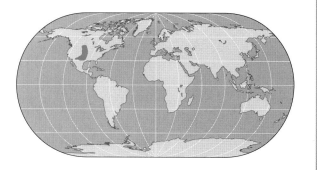

Black-Tailed Prairie Dog

Cynomys ludovicianus

Seemingly empty expanses of land can be home to hundreds of thousands of prairie dogs living in huge, highly organized rodent cities under the ground.

THERE IS NOTHING PARTICULARLY doglike about the appearance of the black-tailed prairie dog and its close relatives: They are in fact members of the squirrel family. However, they are highly social animals, and some of their vocalizations sound a bit like those of small dogs. The most distinctive call is known as the "jump-yip"—a sharp double bark usually given as a territorial warning and accompanied by a sudden half jump in which the animal rears up on its hind legs and flings its "arms" in the air as though trying to shoo the intruder away.

Subterranean Towns

Black-tailed prairie dogs live in huge, highly organized colonies known as "towns." Like human settlements, prairie dog towns vary in size and number of inhabitants. Most cover about 250 acres (100 ha), but they can be much larger. The largest town ever recorded was reputed to cover almost 25,000 square miles (64,750 sq. km) and was home to about 400 million black-tailed prairie dogs—the same as the human populations of the United States and Japan combined!

Within a town there are distinct neighborhoods known as "wards." They can be any size and are usually defined by obvious natural features like banks or clumps of vegetation. Within each ward there are a number of highly territorial family groups called "coteries." They contain eight or nine animals on average, but sometimes more than 20. The coterie is the basic social unit of the prairie dog, and the animals within such a group know each

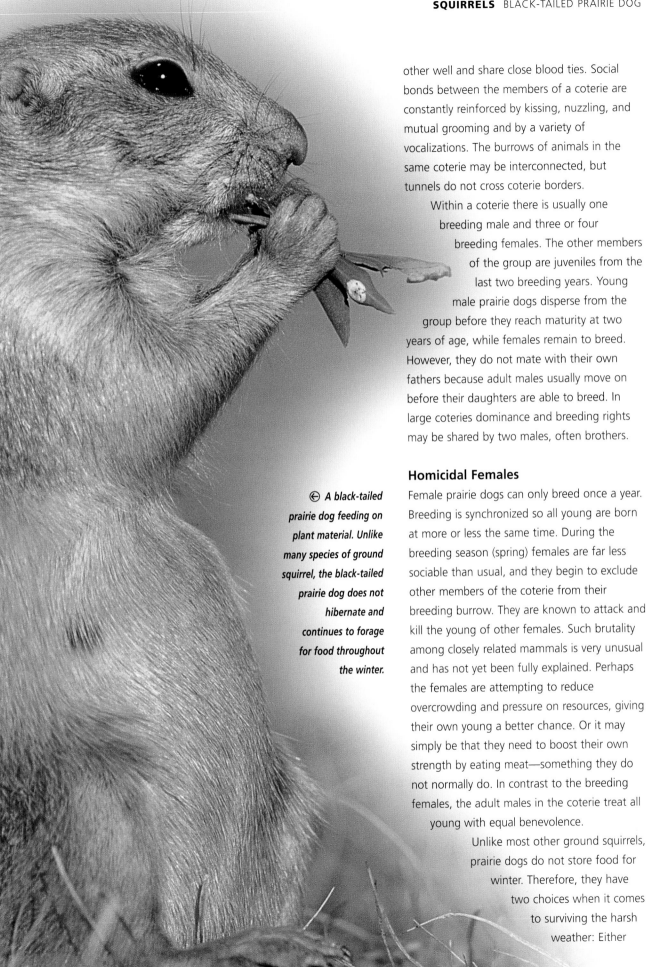

other well and share close blood ties. Social bonds between the members of a coterie are constantly reinforced by kissing, nuzzling, and mutual grooming and by a variety of vocalizations. The burrows of animals in the same coterie may be interconnected, but tunnels do not cross coterie borders.

Within a coterie there is usually one breeding male and three or four breeding females. The other members of the group are juveniles from the last two breeding years. Young male prairie dogs disperse from the group before they reach maturity at two years of age, while females remain to breed. However, they do not mate with their own fathers because adult males usually move on before their daughters are able to breed. In large coteries dominance and breeding rights may be shared by two males, often brothers.

Homicidal Females

Female prairie dogs can only breed once a year. Breeding is synchronized so all young are born at more or less the same time. During the breeding season (spring) females are far less sociable than usual, and they begin to exclude other members of the coterie from their breeding burrow. They are known to attack and kill the young of other females. Such brutality among closely related mammals is very unusual and has not yet been fully explained. Perhaps the females are attempting to reduce overcrowding and pressure on resources, giving their own young a better chance. Or it may simply be that they need to boost their own strength by eating meat—something they do not normally do. In contrast to the breeding females, the adult males in the coterie treat all young with equal benevolence.

Unlike most other ground squirrels, prairie dogs do not store food for winter. Therefore, they have two choices when it comes to surviving the harsh weather: Either

⊖ *A black-tailed prairie dog feeding on plant material. Unlike many species of ground squirrel, the black-tailed prairie dog does not hibernate and continues to forage for food throughout the winter.*

A Home on the Prairie

There is far more to a prairie dog burrow than a simple tunnel in the ground. The burrows are built to precise specifications. Not only are they the perfect size and shape for their owners, but they are also designed with emergency entrances, flood defenses, and built-in air conditioning. Tunnels leading to sleeping chambers are about 4 to 6 inches (10 to 15 cm) in diameter and may extend as far as 100 feet (30 m) underground. Chambers are 12 to 18 inches (30 to 45 cm) across. There is normally more than one entrance, sometimes as many as five or six, and they drop vertically down into the tunnels for easy access. There is usually a shelf or chamber just inside the entrance to make climbing out easier. The soil that is excavated from the burrow is heaped around the entrance, where the prairie dog carefully compacts it and creates a conical mound, like a volcano, with the burrow entrance in the central crater. Having a raised entrance prevents rainwater from running into the hole, and the burrows stay remarkably clean and dry all year round. Because the burrows can be anything from 3 to 16 feet (1 to 5 m) deep, there is a danger of air trapped inside becoming very stale. But having different-sized mounds at each entrance means that when a breeze blows over the ground, air moves faster over some burrow entrances than others. That creates a gentle flow of air in the burrow system and keeps it well ventilated. The burrow is a complicated piece of engineering to understand, and yet the black-tailed prairie dog instinctively knows how to build it.

they remain active and continue to forage for food, or they must hibernate in order to save energy until spring. While the Utah and white-tailed prairie dogs do hibernate, the black-tailed species remains more or less active through the winter. It may remain dormant in its burrow during very cold weather, but rouses regularly to feed and never enters the deep, torpid slumber of true hibernation.

Prairie dogs eat mostly grass and herbaceous vegetation. They forage in a systematic fashion, nibbling the turf in one part of their range very short before moving on and leaving the close-cropped turf for a while to regrow. Regular clipping quickly eliminates tall vegetation and encourages the growth of low, vigorous plants. Prairie dogs never let the grass get long enough to provide cover for larger animals, and so predators such as coyotes or badgers find it impossible to approach unnoticed. Group security is further improved by the members of a coterie taking turns standing guard, often using one of the large burrow entrance mounds as a lookout post. However, there is little doubt that their greatest threat comes from humans.

SEE ALSO Badger, American **1**:76; Coyote **2**:58

Rise and Fall

Early on, the spread of European settlers across the prairies gave a significant boost to the prairie dog population. Pasture created for livestock turned out to be ideal prairie dog habitat and the ranchers obligingly killed or drove away many natural predators. By 1900 there were an estimated 5 billion black-tailed prairie dogs in the United States. However, the species soon became regarded as a menace. Not only do prairie dogs eat a lot of grass, their burrows destabilize the ground, creating a hazard to livestock and a nuisance to farm machinery. In the early part of the 20th century prairie dogs were poisoned by the millions and their towns were plowed up and destroyed. The population today is less than 0.1 percent of what it was 100 years ago, and the majority of surviving colonies live in protected areas such as national parks. Some of the species' close relatives are even more scarce.

⤒ *Two prairie dogs greet each other by pressing nose to nose. Prairie dogs are a social species whose bonds are reinforced by interactions such as nuzzling, "kissing," and grooming.*

⬸ *A black-tailed prairie dog family in Colorado. The family, or "coterie," is the basic social unit of prairie dogs, members of which know each other extremely well.*

59

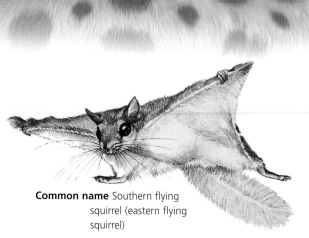

Common name Southern flying squirrel (eastern flying squirrel)

Scientific name *Glaucomys volans*

Family Sciuridae

Order Rodentia

Size Length head/body: 8–9 in (21–24 cm); tail length: 3–4 in (8–10 cm)

Weight 1.7–4 oz (50–120 g)

Key features Small silvery-gray squirrel with bushy but flattened tail and furry gliding membrane stretching from wrists to ankles; head large with big ears and huge black eyes

Habits Nocturnal, social, and gregarious; arboreal; hoards food—does not hibernate; "flies" by gliding on flaps of skin stretched between front and back limbs

Breeding One or 2 litters of 1–6 (usually 2–4) young born in spring and summer after gestation period of 40 days. Weaned at 8–9 weeks; sexually mature at 9 months. May live up to 14 years in captivity, considerably fewer in the wild

Voice Chirping and squeaking calls, many of which are too high-pitched for humans to hear

Diet Nuts, acorns, bark, fungi, fruit, and lichen; occasionally eats insects and meat

Habitat Woodland

Distribution Southeastern Canada, eastern U.S., and Central America south to Honduras

Status Population: abundant. Has declined in some areas due to deforestation, but generally secure; may be responsible for the decline of the related but much rarer northern flying squirrel in some areas

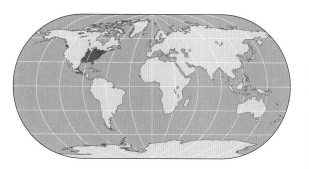

RODENTS

Southern Flying Squirrel
Glaucomys volans

The southern flying squirrel is one of about 30 species of tree-dwelling rodents that have solved the problem of traveling from tree to tree by taking to the air.

AT FIRST GLANCE BABY FLYING squirrels look similar to most other infant rodents—tiny, pink, hairless, and with their eyes and ears sealed over with skin. Their legs are rather long, but closer examination reveals something far more unusual: The babies appear to be wearing skins that are many sizes too big for them. A large fold of skin forms a double membrane that links the wrist to the ankle along each flank. As the baby grows, the extra skin thickens and becomes furred along with the rest of the body. At six or seven weeks of age the young squirrels first emerge from their nest in a tree hole, nest box, or attic. At about eight weeks the purpose of the extra skin suddenly becomes clear: The squirrels can be seen taking to the air like miniature stunt parachutists.

Skillful Pilots

A flying squirrel's "flights" are in fact carefully controlled glides. Before launching itself with a powerful thrust of its back legs, the squirrel examines its distant landing site from several angles, tilting its head this way and that to help gauge distance and trajectory. Once airborne, it opens its gliding membrane by spreading its legs wide. This greatly slows its descent and allows it to travel up to 3 feet (1 m) horizontally for every foot of vertical descent. So from a 60-foot (18-m) perch a squirrel can "fly" up to 150 feet (50 m) to a point well above ground level in another tree. The flattened tail acts as a rudder; and by changing the shape of its parachute, the squirrel can exert fine control over its glide, even swerving in midair. On

landing, the squirrel instantly scurries around the tree trunk in case its glide was noticed by the sharp eyes of an owl.

The southern flying squirrel is the smaller of two closely related species living in North America. However, it is more common than its relative the northern flying squirrel (*Glaucomys sabrinus*) and, despite its diminutive size, appears to be dominant in areas where the distribution of the two species overlaps.

Winter Provisions

Most of the year southern flying squirrels are sociable. They actively seek out each other's company—especially in cold winters, when up to 50 squirrels may be found huddled together in a secure nest. The animals do not hibernate, but they will remain inactive during bad weather. Flying squirrels feed on nuts and acorns, which they gather in large quantities during the fall. They hide the food in nest holes and other nooks and crannies to provide a winter larder.

Male flying squirrels share home ranges all year round. However, during the breeding season females establish a personal territory, which males visit to compete for the right to mate. Females are capable of rearing two litters a year, but that only happens if spring comes relatively early and is more common in southern parts of the species' range.

⊖ *A southern flying squirrel prepares to land on the trunk of a tree. At the last moment it swings its back legs forward so that all four feet land together.*

Common name Indian giant squirrel
(Malabar squirrel, ratufa)

Scientific name *Ratufa indica*

Family   Sciuridae

Order   Rodentia

Size   Length head/body: 14–16 in (35–40 cm); tail
length: up to 24 in (60 cm)

Weight 2.2–6.6 lb (1–3 kg)

Key features Huge squirrel
with glossy black fur on back;
warm buffy-brown below; ears
have obvious neat tufts; tail less bushy than
other tree squirrels and covered in long hair

Habits   Arboreal; usually solitary

Breeding   Litters of 1–2 or more young born after
gestation period of about 4 weeks. Weaned
at 2–3 months; sexually mature at 2 years.
May live up to 20 years in captivity, many
fewer in the wild

Voice   Rapid chattering and soft churring sounds

Diet   Fruit, nuts, bark, and occasional animal
material such as insects and eggs

Habitat   Moist deciduous, mixed, and evergreen forest

Distribution Central and eastern India

Status   Population: unknown; IUCN Vulnerable;
CITES II. Threatened by loss and
fragmentation of habitat

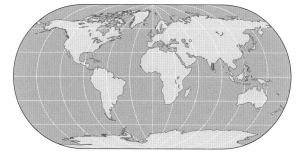

Indian Giant Squirrel

Ratufa indica

There are four species of giant squirrel living in India and Southeast Asia, but sadly, all have suffered serious declines as a result of hunting and habitat loss.

MEASURING UP TO 40 INCHES (102 cm) from head to tail, the Indian giant squirrel is the world's longest squirrel. It is also one of the most arboreal, spending the majority of its life high in the trees of its humid forest home in central and eastern India. It is a handsome animal, with rich dark-brown, almost black fur on its back and flanks and pale-brown underparts. Its tail is long and hairy. The ears have short tufts of black fur. The feet are large but otherwise similar to those of other squirrels, with four long toes on the front paws and five toes on the back. The palms and soles are covered with rough skin to help with grip, and the claws are long, sharp, and strong.

Giant Nests

Indian giant squirrels live alone most of the time, but may associate in breeding pairs. They are rather shy and elusive, and so the precise details of their daily lives are not well known. It is thought that where possible they nest and rear young in large tree holes, although they can also build their own nests out of branches and twigs wedged into the branches of a tree. These nests are more or less spherical and similar to the dreys of typical tree squirrels, except that they are huge—about the size of an eagle's nest. Litters of giant squirrels are small. They usually have only one or two babies, but it is thought that females may be able to rear several such litters a year.

The giant squirrel's large size means there are few branches broad enough for it to sit comfortably back on its haunches to feed as

 SEE ALSO Prairie Dog, Black-Tailed 7:56

back when resting. In most other ways the giant squirrel moves in much the same way as its smaller relatives. It is extremely agile and can scramble along branches and leap from tree to tree with astounding speed. Individual squirrels have been known to jump a massive 25 feet (7.5 m) from one branch to another. They can also travel fast on the ground, although they rarely have cause to do so except when chasing an intruder or potential mate.

Fragmented Habitat

The Indian giant squirrel needs big trees forming extensive forests. Throughout Asia large areas of forest have been felled for fuel or cleared by logging companies seeking to export the valuable timber. Sadly, the Indian giant squirrel and all three of its close relatives are at risk of extinction if current trends continue. While they remain fairly widespread across a large area of India, populations have been broken into hundreds of parts. Many now live in tiny fragments of forest habitat and are unlikely to survive. India is also one of the most intensively cultivated countries in the world, and the pressure for agricultural land to feed its ever-growing human population leaves little room for the conservation of wildlife. Many of the patches of forest where the giant squirrel lives have only been spared because they contain sacred religious sites, but most of them are too small to support a viable population of squirrels.

Under such conditions inbreeding and disease or a season of bad weather could easily wipe out a local population, which because of its isolation will never be replaced. To add to the pressures of habitat loss, giant squirrels are hunted for meat and body parts, some of which are used in traditional medicines.

⊕ *An Indian giant squirrel eats leaves in the rain forest. The health of many forest ecosystems depends on tree squirrels as seed dispersers.*

other squirrels do. Instead, it balances itself on a branch with its head and upper body leaning out on one side, counterbalanced by its long tail hanging over the other. By contrast, smaller tree squirrels carry their tail raised over their

The Mouse and Rat Family

Considering their great numbers, rats and mice (murids) are an extraordinarily conservative group, and many of the more than 1,300 species look virtually identical to the untrained eye. Most murids have the standard rodent arrangement of teeth, with a single pair of large, self-sharpening incisors in the upper and lower jaw. Both pairs are separated from the cheek teeth by an obvious gap. Mice generally have three molars on either side of both jaws. However, the precise structure and arrangement of the teeth vary among the different species. The teeth are therefore useful to scientists, providing the basis for recognition and classification of rats and mice. Common to all murids are powerful masseter muscles, which extend forward from the lower to upper jaw, generating significant gnawing power.

① *Representative species from six groups of New World rats and mice: deer or white-footed mouse (genus Peromyscus) (1); pygmy mouse (genus Baiomys) (2); South American climbing rat (genus Rhipidomys) (3); Central American vesper rat (genus Nyctomys) (4); Central American climbing rat (genus Tylomys) (5).*

Family Muridae: 16 subfamilies, over 280 genera, and more than 1,300 species

Subfamily Murinae (Old World rats and mice): 123 genera

Subfamily Sigmodontinae (New World rats and mice): 79 genera

Subfamily Arvicolinae (voles, muskrats, and lemmings): 26 genera

Subfamily Dendromurinae (African tree-dwelling mice): 8 genera

Subfamily Cricetinae (hamsters and similar rodents): 7 genera

Subfamily Nesomyinae (tufted-tailed rats): 7 genera

Subfamily Cricetomyinae (pouched rats and mice): 3 genera

Subfamily Rhizomyinae (African mole rats and bamboo rats): 3 genera

Subfamily Petromyscinae (rock mice): 2 genera

Subfamily Platacanthomyinae (pygmy dormice): 2 genera

Subfamily Spalacinae (European mole rats): 2 genera

Subfamily Myospalacinae (zokors/mole rat): 1 genus

Subfamily Lophomyinae (African crested rat): 1 genus

Subfamily Calomyscinae (mouselike hamsters): 1 genus

Subfamily Mystromyinae (white-tailed mouse): 1 genus

Subfamily Gerbillinae (gerbils, jirds, and sand rats): 14 genera

Lifestyle

The basic murid body plan is that of a generalist. But to fully exploit the countless ecological niches available to them, many rats and mice have specialized in a huge variety of lifestyles. There are few terrestrial habitats that do not support some kind of mouse or rat.

Climbing mice and rats tend to have long-toed feet for gripping. Some, such as the Asian climbing rats and Indonesian key-footed rats, have opposable thumbs so that they can grip things with their hands. African climbing mice are nimble despite only having three toes on each front foot. They use their tail as a handy fifth limb, and some are so adept in the trees that they may live and breed in old birds' nests. The tails of climbing species are usually long to aid balance. Sometimes they are prehensile, as in European and American harvest mice. The two species are alike in other ways, too. Both are small and build woven nests of grass suspended in tall grass. Yet they owe their similarities not to a recent common ancestor but to convergent evolution. It is the

① *Species of Old World rats and mice: smooth-tailed giant rat (genus* Mallomys) *(1); Natal multimammate rat (genus* Mastomys) *(2); African marsh rat (genus* Dasymys) *(3); pencil-tailed tree mouse (genus* Chiropodomys) *(4); spiny mouse (genus* Acomys) *(5); brush-furred rat (genus* Lophuromys) *(6); vlei rat (genus* Otomys) *(7); Australian water rat (genus* Hydromys) *(8).*

① *Not all Australian mammals are marsupials. Many typical rats and mice also live there, for example, the plains rat (Pseudomys australis). They must now compete with introduced animals for the same resources.*

process by which animals with different evolutionary backgrounds become alike because of sharing a similar lifestyle. Convergence is one reason why classifying mice and rats is an enormously complicated task; animals that appear similar are not necessarily closely related.

Most mice can swim, and several species are as at home in water as they are on land—and find most of their food under water. Adaptations to a semiaquatic lifestyle include a streamlined body, usually with small ears, a waterproof coat, and modifications to the feet and tail. Muskrats, for example, have large hind feet with partial webbing and a fringe of stiff hair. The tail is flattened to make a better rudder. So-called water rats do not form a distinct group within the Muridae. Convergent evolution has created semiaquatic members of several subfamilies, including species of both the Old and New World mice, the voles, and the Australasian water rat.

The basic murid body plan is well suited to life in small spaces, and almost all mice will take advantage of burrows for shelter. The majority are also capable of digging burrows for themselves, but with varying efficiency. Truly fossorial species such as the mole mice of South America and the mole rats of Africa and Eurasia spend almost all their lives underground.

As well as their different habitats and lifestyles, members of the family Muridae also show a wide range of dietary preferences. The kind of food they eat is reflected by differences in the detailed structure of their teeth, especially the molars. Voles and lemmings are basically vegetarian, feeding on mosses, grasses, leaves, and fruit. They have teeth with prominent zigzag patterns on their crowns—highly efficient at shredding coarse vegetation. House mice are the ultimate omnivores and will try eating almost anything. Their teeth have a general-purpose structure, with knobby grinding surfaces much like our own. Some murids are predatory carnivores, for example, the fish-eating rats of South America. Predatory murids generally occupy large home ranges and live at lower densities than other species.

Reproduction

The great reproductive potential of murids is well known and is one reason for the group's success. Many species are able to rear litters in rapid succession because females come into season almost immediately after the birth of their young. This so-called postpartum estrus means that a mother mouse can be suckling one litter while already pregnant with the next. Gestation is usually longer in females that are lactating (producing milk) than in those without young families. As long as weaning time is shorter than gestation, the female will be able to keep producing litter after litter until the end of the season or until she is worn out. Suckling and pregnancy are hard work, and doing both at once puts a huge strain on the female. Mothers are often forced to forage in daylight to find enough food, a risky activity at the best of times and slowed down by the weight of developing young. But the abruptness with which most small murids meet their end is all the more reason to breed fast.

Young mice develop quickly. In the fastest breeding species, the Norway lemming, females can become pregnant before they are even weaned, at just two weeks old. Such fast breeding means the animals can take advantage of short breeding seasons and rapidly build up numbers to exploit empty habitats. However, the boom times are short-lived, and such populations ultimately crash; then the cycle begins again. Other species of rat and mouse have slightly less reckless reproductive strategies. Sometimes not all females are allowed to breed. Dominant females can suppress breeding in others, often their own offspring, by producing chemicals known as pheromones. They inhibit the reproductive cycles of the subordinate females, preventing them from coming into estrus. Female pheromones can also affect male mice, reducing aggression in territorial species. Males produce pheromones, too, and in many species the presence of a mature male is enough to bring females into breeding

condition. Interestingly, the effect is often much stronger if the male is a stranger. In several colonial vole and mouse species the appearance of a new male can trigger spontaneous abortions in pregnant females. The females immediately come into estrus again and mate with the new male. By breeding with strange males, females reduce the probability of inbreeding within a colony.

Balancing the Numbers

In most species high birthrates are balanced by equally high death rates, and life expectancy for any one mouse or rat is generally short. Apart from overcrowding and starvation, predation is the main factor limiting population growth in most species. The incisor teeth, while long and sharp, are not designed for fighting, and a mouse can do little more to defend itself than nip a larger animal. A few mice have evolved a limited defense in the form of spines that grow like extrathick, stiff hairs among the fur on the animal's back. The tree-dwelling Kenyan crested rat (Lophiomys imhausi) has a mane of long hairs running down its back, which it raises when threatened. Some of the longer hairs look rather like the spines of a porcupine. If the predator has already learned that porcupinelike animals are not good prey, the crested rat's bluff may well be enough to deter an attack.

Mice and Humans

Their vast numbers, adaptability, and speed of reproduction mean that some species of murids can become serious pests. They devour growing crops and stored food and multiply alarmingly. Rats—and some mice—also spread diseases, some of which can be fatal. Rats and mice have been hailed as the biggest threat to the human economy posed by any mammals. However, modern poisons may have exterminated them locally in parts of Europe and North America. On the other hand, laboratory mice have played a major role in scientific research and disease control.

➔ *The fierce-tempered golden-backed tree rat (Mesembriomys macrurus) is found in the northern parts of Western Australia and the far north of the Northern Territory. It nests in the Pandanus palm.*

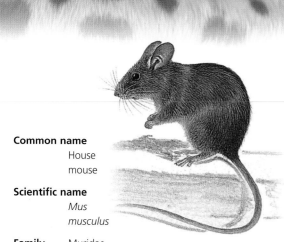

Common name
House mouse

Scientific name
Mus musculus

Family Muridae

Order Rodentia

Size Length head/body: 3–4.5 in (8–11 cm); tail length: 3–4 in (8–10 cm)

Weight 0.5–1 oz (14–28 g)

Key features Small, slim body; pointed face with large, sparsely haired ears; long, scaly pink tail; fur grayish-brown, often greasy and smelly

Habits Generally nocturnal; often aggressive; excellent climber, also swims well; lives wild and in association with people

Breeding Up to 14 litters of 4–10 young born at any time of year after gestation period of 19–21 days (more if female is suckling previous litter). Weaned at 3 weeks; sexually mature at 6 weeks. May live up to 6 years in captivity, 2 in the wild

Voice Squeaks

Diet Omnivorous: almost anything of plant or animal origin, including leather, wax, cloth, soap, and paper; also chews man-made materials such as plastics and synthetic fabrics

Habitat Farms, food supplies, fields, and houses

Distribution Almost worldwide

Status Population: billions. Less common than previously in many developed countries due to intensive pest control and mouse-proof buildings

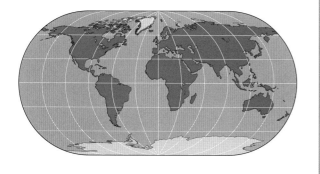

House Mouse *Mus musculus*

The house mouse is a familiar animal all over the world. Ecologically it is a "Jack-of-all-trades," and its generalist lifestyle has allowed it to make a living anywhere that people can.

TRADITIONAL STORIES AND CARTOON animations would have us believe that the sight of a house mouse is enough to send housewives (and their husbands, too) shrieking onto the nearest stool. Despite their reputation, house mice are not really that exciting to look at. In fact, they are drab little animals, with coarse, grayish-brown fur, which is almost always slightly greasy, not sleek and dry like that of a wood mouse. The house mouse smells musty and rather unpleasant, and it moves like greased lightning, but it is not entirely without charm. It has bright black eyes, large charismatic ears, and an inquisitive, twitchy nose. All in all, it is difficult to see why anyone should be frightened of one.

Association with Humans

The house mouse first appeared on the steppes of Central Asia, but is now one of the world's most widespread mammals. It lives wild in deserts, swamps, hedgerows, and forests, from the sweltering tropics to windswept islands. However, the house mouse's big break in terms of conquering the world was undoubtedly its association with humans. House mice can live anywhere that people can, from cities to Antarctic research stations, coal mines to mountain huts. They can be found in subways and public buildings, and are even known to take up residency in the finest hotels.

House mice do best in traditionally managed farmland, where large quantities of crops or animal feed are stored in barns. In such a place mouse populations can increase spectacularly. When the owner of one such farm in Australia began a poisoning campaign to control the mice, he awoke next morning to find almost 30,000 corpses on his doorstep.

⬆ *A house mouse feeding on blackberries growing in a hedgerow. The diet of house mice is exceptionally varied and can include such items as wax and soap.*

 SEE ALSO Rat, Brown **7**:72; Mouse, Wood **7**:78

Mouse Proof

For most people living in towns and cities in the developed world, the scourge of the house mouse is no longer really a reality. Modern building technology and food storage facilities mean that most homes are pretty much mouse proof, and mouse problems are easily dealt with by poisoning. It is known that in some places mice have become resistant to certain poisons that are used to control them, but there are more being developed all the time. As a result, mouse infestations are now little more than a nuisance in many parts of the world. Mice have a way of getting into all kinds of unexpected places. They wreak havoc by chewing fabrics, paperwork, and even electrical cables.

Singing and Dancing Mice

House mice have been specially bred to make pets and laboratory animals. There are many different strains, some of which are distinctive enough to have been given names. "Shaker" and "waltzing" mice actually have something wrong with the part of their nervous system that controls balance, meaning they cannot walk properly. Shaker mice weave and wobble as they walk, while waltzers seem to run in constant dizzying circles, going nowhere fast. Under normal circumstances such defects would be catastrophic to individuals, but sometimes life is so easy for house mice that afflicted animals are still able to get by and reproduce.

So-called "singing mice" habitually make twittering sounds that can be heard from some distance away. Drawing attention to themselves would be disastrous for most small animals—and no doubt any wild singing mice would meet a sticky end if overheard by a cat or weasel. However, in the relative safety of human habitations the mice can often breed fast enough that some survive to pass on their noisy genes. Singing mice have also been specially bred as novelty pets.

House Mouse Behavior

The social behavior of house mice varies depending on their circumstances. At high population densities they do not always defend territories, but often when living alongside humans they become distinctly territorial. Male mice are more aggressive than females and will fight viciously in order to establish dominance. A male shares his territory with several females, with whom he mates. The females have a dominance hierarchy of their own, but it is more peacefully maintained. Both females and young mice help the dominant male repel intruders from the family territory.

House mice mark their territory with smelly droppings and urine. Sometimes the feces accumulate as little stinking pyramids where generations of mice have deposited their messages in the same place. The copious droppings and urine contaminate food, hay, and bedding materials. The mice also gnaw packages, wood, wires, and even lead shot, greatly adding to the economic losses they cause by simply eating stored food.

Apart from its extraordinary adaptability and ability to feed on almost anything, a large

⊙ *Two-week-old mice huddle together in a nest. There are usually four to 10 young per litter and up to 14 litters in a year.*

part of the house mouse's success is due to its reproductive strategy. Female house mice are able to breed when they are just six weeks old. From then on they can produce increasingly large litters roughly once a month for about a year. The offspring mature quickly, but tend not to breed themselves until they have dispersed far enough away from their mother. If they do not move on, they remain under the influence of special chemicals (pheromones) that inhibit ovulation. Inbreeding can lead to birth defects and weakened immune systems, but the pheromones produced by the mother prevent young females from breeding with their own father or other closely related males. It is the combination of rapid breeding and dispersal that enables the house mouse to exploit new opportunities and spread so quickly.

Once established in a breeding range, house mice can be highly sedentary. Studies of mice in grain silos have shown that many individuals never wander more than a couple of yards from their nests. Everything they need is easily found in a small area, and they do not even need to drink where there is ample water in their food. Away from human habitation, house mice are a little more venturesome, traveling several hundred yards in a night and sometimes dispersing more than a mile.

All house mice are incredibly agile. They can climb branches, ropes,

walls, and cables, and they are able to squeeze through minute gaps and under doors. They can also run fast, about 8 miles an hour (13 km/h), faster than the average human jogger several hundred times their size.

Local Varieties

Although they are descended from a relatively recent shared ancestor, house mice in different parts of the world show distinct regional variations. Many local varieties are now classified as subspecies of *Mus musculus*.

Some of the differences between the subspecies can be used to trace the routes by which the house mouse has conquered the world. The closest thing to the ancestor of all house mice is thought to be a subspecies called *Mus musculus wagneri*, which originated in the steppe county between the Black and Caspian Seas. Interestingly, the area also contains evidence of the earliest arable farming: Its people started cultivating

cereal crops several thousand years ago. No doubt the mice took advantage of stored grain, thus forming a relationship with humans that has continued to this day. Mice were unwittingly transported with grain being traded east and west, and by 4,000 years ago they had spread to Europe and North Africa. By 1200 B.C. there were house mice in Britain, and by medieval times there were two distinct subspecies in northern and southern Europe.

The southern subspecies (*Mus musculus brevirostris*) made it to South and Central America and California with the Spanish and Portuguese conquistadors. At the same time, the northern variety (*Mus musculus musculus*) was colonizing North America along with the Pilgrim Fathers. Nowadays a large proportion of western Europe has been taken over by another subspecies (*Mus musculus domesticus*), which is characterized by a longer tail.

⊕ *A house mouse feeds on grain stored in a sack. Wherever cereal crops are cultivated, house mice also thrive. The species' relationship with humans can be traced back to the earliest arable farming, several thousand years ago.*

Common name Brown rat (common rat, Norway rat)

Scientific name *Rattus norvegicus*

Family	Muridae
Order	Rodentia
Size	Length head/body: 9–11 in (22–29 cm); tail length: 7–9 in (17–23 cm)

Weight 9–28 oz (255–790 g)

Key features	Typical rat with short legs, longish fingers and toes, and pointed face; ears pink and prominent; scaly tail noticeably shorter than head and body; fur dull grayish-brown, fading to white or pale gray on belly
Habits	Generally nocturnal; social; cautious at first but can become bold; climbs and swims well
Breeding	Up to 12 litters of 1–22 (usually 8 or 9) young born at any time of year (but mostly in spring and summer) after gestation period of 21–26 days. Weaned at 3 weeks; sexually mature at 2–3 months. May live up to 6 years in captivity, 3 in the wild
Voice	Loud squeaks when frightened or angry
Diet	Anything edible, including fruit, grain, meat, eggs, wax, and soap; will catch and kill other small animals
Habitat	Almost anywhere food can be found
Distribution	Worldwide in association with humans; not normally in more sparsely populated areas of the world
Status	Population: several billion

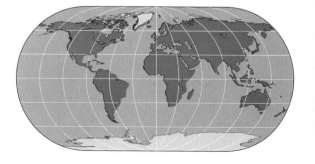

Brown Rat

Rattus norvegicus

The brown rat is one of the most successful mammals on the planet. It rivals humans in terms of distribution and number, and continues to exploit us successfully despite our best efforts to exterminate it.

THE BROWN RAT IS PERHAPS the most reviled of all mammals. Even the word "rat" has all kinds of meanings, every one of them negative. Someone in a bad mood is described as "ratty," we detect wrongdoing when we "smell a rat," and telling tales to get someone else into trouble is "ratting."

Rats have few friends in spite of the fact that the vast majority of species are totally harmless. The brown rat is one the largest of 56 species in the genus *Rattus*, most of which live completely wild and never trouble people at all. But such is the strength of the brown rat's bad reputation worldwide that virtually all rats and ratlike rodents are treated as vermin.

Eastern Origins

Despite the misleading alternative name of Norway rat, the brown rat is thought to have originated in India or northern China. It spread to Europe and the Americas less quickly than its more inquisitive cousin, the ship rat, but today it is the dominant commensal rat species in most temperate parts of the world. In many places it has displaced the ship rat altogether. Brown rats prefer to live on the ground rather than in trees, and their liking for wet places suggests that their natural habitat may once have been stream banks. Brown rats swim well and are often associated with canals, sewers, and irrigation systems. They are expert at catching fish. They are also proficient diggers, and in the wild they create extensive burrow systems with many entrances and chambers.

The diet of brown rats can be extraordinarily diverse. They even manage to survive on the debris of seashores. Given a choice, however, they seem to prefer eating

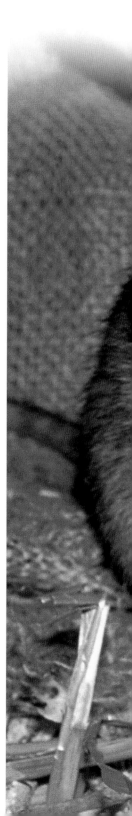

SEE ALSO Rat, Ship 7:76

meat and animal matter to fruit and grains. Their teeth are relatively unspecialized: They use their incisors for gnawing and their molars for grinding fragments of food. In association with humans rats will eat almost anything, including soap, wax, leather, and paper. They thrive in cities, where drains provide them with shelter and food. Litter and overflowing trashcans offer all kinds of high-energy fatty foods loved by humans and rats alike. Food is often so abundant that an urban brown rat can spend its entire adult life in a home range as little as 80 to 500 feet (24 to 150 m) across.

The social structure of brown rats is rather variable, with the level of organization depending on the density of the local population. At low densities dominant males defend territories within which several females will collectively and cooperatively rear his offspring. If all available territories are taken, the excess rats form large gangs within which many males try to mate with every estrous female. Aggression is rife, there is no fixed dominance structure, and the stresses of life mean that reproductive success is low compared with that in the well-organized world of the territory-holding rats.

Brown rats can feed on a wide variety of foods. They are a versatile species and can make their living almost anywhere there is human habitation.

Rapid Breeders

Under good conditions brown rats can breed prolifically. A single pair can, in theory, multiply to over 15,000 animals in the space of a year. Rapid increases in population cannot be sustained for long, however, and brown rat numbers tend to fluctuate considerably. Overcrowding either leads to population crashes caused by starvation or disease, or to sudden mass dispersions, with thousands of rats suddenly on the move.

Brown rats will fight fiercely for their lives and will attack dogs, cats, and even people if cornered. There are even reports of brown rats killing babies and helpless humans by biting them continuously until they bleed to death. Of course, such incidents are extremely rare, but they add to the rat's evil reputation.

It surprises most people to discover that brown rats are actually quite clean animals. Wherever possible they take pains

to groom themselves using their tongue, teeth, and claws to wash and scrape dirt from their fur. They cover their palms in saliva to wipe their face and whiskers clean. However, such is the filth in some of the man-made environments they frequent, it is virtually impossible for some rats to ever get fully clean. It is true that rats carry many diseases that can infect people. Rabies, typhus, Weil's disease, rat-bite fever, and food poisoning (*Salmonella*) are just a few of the more serious infections known to be spread by brown rats.

Pest Control

The battle to control rats has been running for centuries. People have been employed as rat catchers since the Middle Ages, and there were dogs trained specifically for the task. The legend of the Pied Piper of Hamelin tells how the mysterious piper led the town rats to their deaths in the local river, having bewitched them with his music. When the townspeople refused to pay him, the piper took revenge by piping away all their children, who were never seen again. The rats in the story were probably ship rats rather than brown rats, but either way it normally takes more than music to rid a town of rat infestations. However, rats are vulnerable to poisoning. They cannot vomit; so even if they realize something is making them ill, they cannot void it from their stomach. One of the earliest rat poisons

Ⓣ *The fairytale of the Pied Piper of Hamelin tells of a piper who charmed the rats away from the German town with his mysterious music.*

→ *A brown rat carries an infant. The young are born blind and naked but are quick developers—after just three weeks they are ready to leave the nest.*

Even Rats Have Their Uses

Albino brown rats are naturally more docile than their full-color relatives. After generations of selective breeding they have become exceedingly tame and are widely used in medical and scientific research. Twenty million white rats are used in United States labs every year. Some are bred with specific weaknesses so that medical researchers can assess the efficacy of various new therapies. Others are used in experiments on physiology, neurology, genetics, behavior, and psychology. Brown rats have even been into space. In 1960 two lab rats spent time in orbit aboard a Russian satellite and returned to earth apparently none the worse for their adventure.

was derived from a plant called Mediterranean squill. Eaten by a human or a dog, it causes severe nausea and vomiting, but in rats it causes paralysis and death. However, rats are smart, and once one rat has been poisoned by something, others in the colony will avoid eating the same thing. Also, rats will not eat anything that has made them feel ill before, so slow-acting or cumulative poisons are no use. Brown rats are also naturally suspicious of anything new. Ship rats are less cautious, which is one reason why poisoning campaigns have been more effective with that species.

Death Sentence

A breakthrough in rodenticide technology came in 1950 with the development of a poison called warfarin. Warfarin contains dicoumarol, a small dose of which causes massive internal bleeding and death. Most importantly, the rats are unable to detect warfarin in foods and so do not learn to avoid it. Nor do they learn from others' mistakes, because death occurs some time after the poison is eaten. Yet as early as 1958 there were examples of rats that were apparently unharmed by dicoumarol, and the percentage of resistant rats is growing. The development of new poisons continues.

⊕ *An albino brown rat in a piece of laboratory equipment being used in a toxicology test.*

Common name Ship rat (black rat, house rat, roof rat, plague rat)

Scientific name *Rattus rattus*

Family Muridae

Order Rodentia

Size Length head/body: 6–9.5 in (15–24 cm); tail length: 4.5–12 in (12–30 cm)

Weight 5–10 oz (150–280 g)

Key features Slender body with long, scaly tail; face pointed; hairless ears larger than those of brown rat; fur black or gray-brown

Habits Nocturnal; social; excellent climber; a pest of stored foodstuffs; often associated with human habitation, especially around ports and on ships

Breeding Up to 5 litters of 1–16 (usually 7 or 8) young born at any time of year after gestation period of 21–29 days. Weaned at 3 weeks; sexually mature at 2–4 months. May live up to 4 years in captivity, 2 in the wild

Voice Loud squeaks and whistles

Diet Varied; all kinds of foods stored by humans, especially fond of fruit

Habitat Varied; forests and farmland, but does well in towns

Distribution Originally from India; now found along tropical and temperate coasts of all continents except Antarctica

Status Population: many millions. Increasingly rare due to intensive persecution, but unlikely to receive protection because of bad reputation

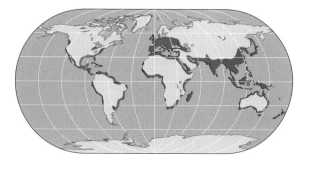

Ship Rat

Rattus rattus

"Ship rat" seems an odd name for an animal with an inherent dislike of water, but it is apt nonetheless. Without human conquest of the world's oceans the ship rat may never have earned its notoriety.

BOLD AND LESS CAUTIOUS THAN its brown cousin, the ship rat is also extremely agile. Having spread into Europe along trade routes from the Far East and India, it fearlessly boarded ships via mooring lines—or in the cargo itself—without ever having to get its dainty toes wet. As a result, the ship rat spread much faster than the brown rat, arriving in Britain with the Romans and in the Americas with some of the earliest European settlers in the mid-16th century. Once ashore, the ship rat lives higher up than the brown rat, preferring buildings and attics to sewers and garbage dumps.

Group Dynamics

Ship rats live in social groups dominated by a single adult male. Subordinate males form a hierarchy under the chief, but they are also dominated by the top females. All members of the group help defend the group territory, but males are usually tolerant of intruding females (which they view as possible mates rather than potential rivals). Dominant females are highly aggressive. Breeding females rear families in nests of shredded vegetation, cloth, or paper located in secure sites well off the ground.

Ship rats eat almost anything. They can cause immense damage to stored crops, especially coconuts, sugarcane, and grain. As well as eating the crops, they contaminate them with droppings and urine. They also eat the eggs and young of birds and have been responsible for wiping out whole populations of seabirds from some small islands. Worst of all, perhaps, the ship rat spreads bubonic plague. Plague is caused by a bacterium called *Yersinia pestis* carried by rat fleas. The "Black Death" and "Great Plague" of Europe (in the 13th and

 SEE ALSO Rat, Brown 7:72

17th centuries) killed a quarter of the human population of that continent. As carriers of the fleas, the rats got the blame. In the last century outbreaks of plague have killed 120 million people, mostly in Africa and the Indian subcontinent. The last outbreak in the United States was in Los Angeles in 1924.

The story of the ship rat may yet have a twist in its long tail. Rigorous persecution and competition with the brown or Norway rat, especially in temperate zones, has led to a dramatic decline in ship rat populations in many parts of the world. Their greater curiosity and preference for buildings makes them easier to poison than brown rats. In many countries the species now exists in such small, fragmented populations that it may disappear altogether. Furthermore, recent reinvestigation of historical evidence suggests that the Black Death may not have been caused by bubonic plague at all, but by another equally infectious disease such as anthrax. If so, the ship rat is innocent of the greatest of its alleged crimes. Such new evidence might go some way to improving the animal's public image. Signs that this is already happening include the designation of the ship rat as an Endangered species in Virginia.

Conservation Dilemma

The ship rat is still abundant in many places; but if eradication programs continue at their current rate, the ship rat could be gone from many areas in a matter of decades. Whether or not we should allow that to happen is one of the more difficult decisions facing mammal conservationists in the 21st century.

⊕ *Ship rats are famed pillagers of stored vegetables and grains. Each year they destroy between 5 and 10 percent of China's stored grain.*

Common name Wood mouse
(long-tailed field
mouse)

Scientific name *Apodemus sylvaticus*

Family Muridae

Order Rodentia

Size Length head/body: 3.5–4 in (9–10 cm); tail
length: 3–4.5 in (7–11.5 cm)

Weight 0.5–1 oz (14–28 g)

Key features Small, neat-looking mouse with rounded
body, large ears, large black eyes, and very
long tail; fur golden-brown; white on belly

Habits Nocturnal or crepuscular; more social in
winter than summer; climbs and jumps well;
burrows and stores food

Breeding Up to 4 litters of 2–9 (usually 4–7) young
born spring to fall (season varies with climatic
region) after gestation period of 19–20 days.
Weaned at 18–20 days; sexually mature at 2
months. May live 3–4 years in captivity, rarely
more than 20 months in the wild

Voice Squeaks

Diet Omnivorous: seeds, buds, shoots, fruit, fungi,
and nuts; also snails, insects (especially grubs
and caterpillars), and other arthropods;
cereals such as corn and oats

Habitat Woodland, farmland, scrubland, and gardens;
also mountains and sand dunes

Distribution Iceland, British Isles, most of mainland
Europe (except northern Scandinavia) east to
Central Asia and south to Persian Gulf; also
northwestern Africa

Status Population: abundant

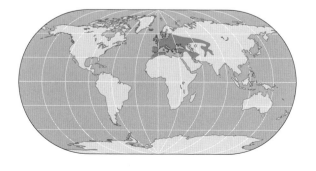

Wood Mouse

Apodemus sylvaticus

*The wood mouse (sometimes
known as the field mouse) is the
most familiar wild mouse
throughout most of Europe.*

THE WOOD MOUSE IS A VERSATILE and adaptable
rodent that lives happily in a variety of habitats,
including woodlands, forests, fields, and
hedgerows. It can also be found well away from
trees, on mountain slopes and sand dunes. It
frequents parks and gardens, and in some
places it is more common in houses and
outbuildings than the house mouse. Wood mice
are the European equivalent of the versatile and
widespread deer mice of North America.

Wholesome Public Image

Wood mice are attractive animals, with a clean,
silky coat, large ears, and twinkling black eyes.
They lack the musty, unpleasant smell
associated with house mice; and although they
can cause a nuisance by nibbling at seed bags
and stored groceries, they generally have a
more wholesome public image. In spring they
eat large quantities of caterpillars and other
insect grubs, providing a service to gardeners
and farmers that goes some way to compensate
for the crops they damage later in the year.

Wood mice are agile climbers, and much of
their natural food is collected from trees and
shrubs. The long, lightly furred tail is not
prehensile like that of the harvest mouse, but is
nevertheless important in maintaining balance
and controlling long leaps. The wood mouse is
preyed on by owls and other birds of prey, and
by weasels, stoats, snakes, foxes, and domestic
cats. Even badgers will dig up breeding nests
and devour the contents. Not surprisingly, wood
mice are wary creatures. They generally emerge
only after dark and, if possible, stay hidden on
bright moonlit nights.

⊖ *The wood mouse inhabits a wide variety of habitats from forests to sand dunes.*

Wood mice are highly active animals. Female home ranges are small, generally only 660 feet (200 m) across. However, in the course of a night's foraging a wood mouse may travel a considerable distance, crisscrossing her range many times. Males are more wide-ranging than females. Their ranges may cover over 7.5 acres (3 ha) and overlap with those of several potential mates. Only breeding females are territorial. They will admit males for mating purposes, but once pregnant or suckling a litter, they drive out any intruders.

Male wood mice may live in groups, sharing a communal nest in a burrow all year round. The nests are generally made of grass and other plants. In winter they are joined by females. Up to a dozen mice may sleep snuggled together, benefiting from shared body warmth. They do not hibernate, although they may allow their body temperature to fall in order to save energy.

Fluctuating Populations

Wood mouse populations can fluctuate greatly from season to season and year to year. Late winter and spring are the toughest times, since reserves of food stored the previous fall begin to run out. Prolonged bouts of cold weather make going out to find more both difficult and dangerous. But if spring comes early, the mice begin to breed right away, and there may be time for healthy females to rear as many as 35 young in the year.

The young of early litters are able to breed even before the summer is over. By the fall there can be large numbers of mice, providing a glut of food for predatory birds and mammals. In a good year there may be over 60 mice per acre (150 per ha). Young wood mice can be easily recognized, since they are gray all over. They suffer heavy mortality with the first cold, wet nights of winter, and most of the smaller, weaker animals of the litter die.

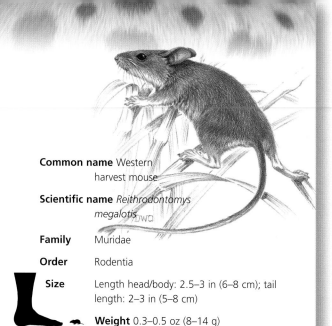

Common name Western harvest mouse

Scientific name *Reithrodontomys megalotis*

Family Muridae

Order Rodentia

Size Length head/body: 2.5–3 in (6–8 cm); tail length: 2–3 in (5–8 cm)

Weight 0.3–0.5 oz (8–14 g)

Key features Tiny mouse with brown fur; white underside; tail long, thin, and sparsely furred; ears large; incisor teeth have prominent grooves

Habits Nocturnal; can be solitary or social; excellent climber; does not hibernate

Breeding Several litters of 1–9 (usually 3–5) young born March–November, occasionally also in winter, after gestation period of 21 days. Weaned at 21 days; sexually mature at 17 weeks. May live up to 30 months in captivity, 18 in the wild

Voice High-pitched "buzzing" calls

Diet Seeds and green shoots, especially grasses

Habitat Short prairie grass, sagebrush desert, pasture, light woodland, and salt marsh

Distribution Southern Alberta and British Columbia; central and western U.S. south to Indiana and central Mexico

Status Population: abundant. Agricultural deforestation has allowed species range to expand since European settlement of North America

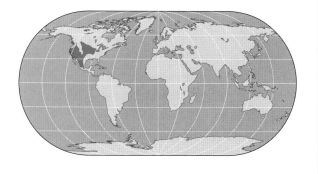

Western Harvest Mouse

Reithrodontomys megalotis

Often the only obvious sign of western harvest mouse activity is their baseball-sized nests of woven grass. The animals themselves are secretive, nocturnal, and extremely small.

WESTERN HARVEST MICE LIVE IN a diverse array of habitats throughout their large range, from semiarid sagebrush scrub to green pasture and the dense vegetation of wooded ravines. Population density varies considerably with habitat and season, from fewer than one mouse per acre to 18 or more per acre (45 per ha). The best habitats are marginal ones. They include the edges of small wooded areas within lightly grazed pastureland, somewhere with a mild temperate climate. Such places provide the mice with a range of foods that come into season at different times of year: green shoots and flowers in spring, seed heads in summer and fall, and a variety of seasonal insects.

Surviving Winter

Winter can be a lean time for harvest mice, and indeed for most rodents, but the harvest mice store seeds to help them through. They are also capable of short periods of torpor during very cold weather. Torpor is a deep sleep during which the mouse's body temperature drops and its metabolism slows down, thereby saving energy. In winter several mice will share a nest in order to conserve body heat. Such behavior is most common in northern individuals.

The western harvest mouse is the second smallest rodent in Canada, where it is at the very northern limit of its range. Its tiny body simply cannot retain enough heat to survive long, harsh winters. The Canadian population is restricted to the extreme southwest and is small and thinly distributed. Elsewhere, however, the western harvest mouse is thriving, and the species has expanded its distributional range in the last 200 years. When European settlers began clearing large expanses of forest in the central states for crops and pasture, they also unwittingly created huge areas of new harvest-mouse habitat. In some areas the benefit has been lost by the introduction of intensive agriculture or by overgrazing, but elsewhere the mice continue to do well.

Other American harvest mouse species are faring less well. Some, such as the Cozumel Island harvest mouse (*R. spectabilis*) and the Costa Rican harvest mouse (*R. rodriguezi*), are facing imminent extinction. Others, including Mexico's hairy harvest mouse (*R. hirsutus*) and

⊕ The western harvest mouse inhabits the grassland areas of western North America, emerging at night to eat grain or seeds and living in a globular nest off the ground in tall grass.

the Nicaraguan harvest mouse (*R. paradoxus*), are cause for concern, having been designated Lower Risk: near threatened by the IUCN.

Woven Nests

American harvest mouse nests consist of a sphere of intricately woven grass stems with a tiny entrance hole on the underside. The nest is lined with soft plant fibers and fluff. There may be several such nests within a home range, usually somewhere safe, like a hollow log or the abandoned burrow of another small mammal; harvest mice do not dig burrows of their own.

Western harvest mice are vulnerable to all kinds of mammal, bird, and reptile predators. They do their best to avoid detection by being strictly nocturnal. They will not even venture out on bright moonlit nights in case they are seen. When moving around their home range, they use regular runways and tunnels through the vegetation. They are agile climbers and will run up trees and shrubs in search of flowers and seeds.

Common name Deer
mouse
(white-footed mouse)

Scientific name *Peromyscus maniculatus*

Family   Muridae

Order   Rodentia

Size   Length head/body: 2.5–4 in (7–10 cm); tail
length: 2–5 in (5–12 cm)

Weight 0.4–1 oz (11–28 g)

Key features Russet-bodied mouse with white underside
and legs; tail 2-tone and variable in length;
head large with huge, sparsely furred, round
ears; black eyes and long whiskers

Habits   Mostly nocturnal; stores food for winter; does
not enter full hibernation

Breeding   Three to 4 litters of 1–9 young born in spring
and summer in north of range (anytime in
south) after gestation period of 22–30 days.
Weaned at 3–4 weeks; females sexually
mature at 6 weeks, males rarely breed before
6 months. May live up to 8 years in captivity,
rarely more than 2 in the wild

Voice   Squeaks and buzzing sounds; drums forefeet
on ground when excited

Diet   Omnivorous: seeds and grains, fruit, flowers,
and other plant material; also insects and
other invertebrates

Habitat   Varied; includes scrubland, prairie, desert,
alpine areas, boreal forest, and woodland

Distribution All of North America except tundra regions
of Canada and southeastern U.S; also Mexico

Status   Population: very abundant

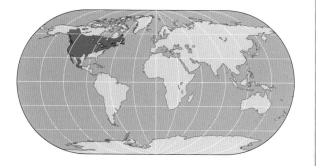

Deer Mouse *Peromyscus maniculatus*

*The deer mouse is the most widespread member
of its genus. It is among the world's more numerous
mammals, producing up to four large litters a year.*

THERE ARE OVER 50 SPECIES OF DEER mouse living in
North and Central America, all of which belong
to the genus *Peromyscus*. Many of them are
similar and can only be told apart biochemically
or by differences in the structure of their
chromosomes. Others are geographically
distinct. For example, a dozen or more are
found only on small islands. At least one species
of deer mouse has recently gone extinct, and
several others are extremely rare.

Continuous Breeders

The common deer mouse, *Peromyscus
maniculatus,* has no such survival worries. It
occupies a huge range, including most of North
America. In some years it is so abundant that it
has been a severe nuisance to the forestry
industry, nibbling seedlings and buds.
Population booms usually follow so-called
"mast years," during which trees such as oak
produce a massive glut of nuts or acorns (mast).
The excess food is stored by mice and many
other animals and consumed over the following
winter, boosting the survival rate. The mice may
even continue to breed all winter long. They are
in good condition in spring and can begin
breeding early. Numbers rapidly build up as the
progeny themselves begin to breed too.

Deer mice can reproduce extremely fast. A
healthy wild female can rear four litters of up to
nine babies a year, and her daughters can
themselves breed before they are two months
old. In captivity, where unlimited food and other
luxuries make life easy for the mice, females can
raise over 100 babies a year.

Every population boom is inevitably
followed by a sharp decline. When a population
crash happens, the mice spread out and
become less social. Females in particular
become partially territorial; and when food is

scarce, they may try to kill each other's offspring. Feeding on young deer mice not only provides mother mice with a good meal, but it reduces the potential competition for her own family. Such rivalry between females is soon forgotten once winter rolls around again, and up to a dozen mice of all ages and sexes will nest together in order to share body warmth.

Wild deer mice are sociable creatures; and when the population booms, they will happily share home ranges. Mothers and daughters will even rear their young in the same nests. On such occasions the baby mice can end up being suckled by their mother, grandmother, aunt, or sister. Male deer mice often get involved in the care of their offspring too. They keep a careful eye on the young, retrieving any that wander off, and help keep the nest clean.

Deer mice are fastidious when it comes to matters of hygiene. Once a nest becomes soiled, they will leave it and build another. Nests are usually woven from grass and other plant material and lined with soft fibers such as thistledown. They are usually wedged into a secure spot such as a tree hole, disused burrow, or dense clump of vegetation.

Popular Laboratory Animals

The docile nature and clean habits of deer mice, along with their rapid rate of reproduction and nonspecialized diet, make them easy to keep in captivity. From a scientist's point of view they are ideal laboratory animals. The closely related white-footed mouse, *Peromyscus leucopus*, has been used as a model to investigate how male and female mammals compete to maximize their breeding success.

⊕ Deer mice spend the day in burrows or trees. Occasionally, they come into buildings, where they nest in mattress stuffing or other soft material. On cold days they may enter a deep, torpid sleep, but they do not hibernate.

Common name
Desert
wood rat (pack rat, trade rat)

Scientific name *Neotoma lepida*

Family Muridae

Order Rodentia

Size Length head/body: 6–9 in (15–23 cm); tail length: 0.5 in (1 cm)

Weight 0.4–1 lb (0.2–0.5 kg)

Key features Brownish-gray rat with pale underside and feet; ears round; furry tail up to half length of body

Habits Nocturnal, solitary, and timid; constructs large "houses" above ground, collecting building material from wide area; does not hibernate

Breeding Two or 3 litters of 1–5 young born at any time of year after gestation period of 30–40 days. Weaned at 4 weeks; sexually mature at 2 months. May live up to 7 years in captivity, several years in the wild

Voice Generally silent

Diet Leaves, seeds, roots, and fleshy cactus pads; also insects and other small invertebrates

Habitat Desert

Distribution Deserts of southwestern U.S. and northwestern Mexico, including Baja California

Status Population: abundant

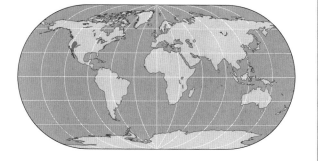

Desert Wood Rat *Neotoma lepida*

One of North America's most charismatic rodents, the timid desert wood rat has earned a place in folklore with its industrious building and sense of fair trade.

THE WOOD RAT'S ALTERNATIVE NAME of pack or trade rat refers to the species' most intriguing behavior. Like most rodents, wood rats are inquisitive and opportunistic. They will help themselves to almost any item of food or other useful object they come across and are always on the lookout for new pieces of building material to add to their elaborate nests.

Honest Traders
Bits of twig, cactus spines, and small bones are all useful nest-building materials. They are collected from all over the rat's home range, an area of about 4,400 square feet (400 sq. m). Wood rats are also very fond of bright, shiny objects, such as foil, silver cutlery, and glass, and will requisition such objects from campsites and gardens. Their habit of collecting objects is not unusual, since rodents are well-known thieves. Where the wood rat differs is that it often appears to "pay" for what it takes by leaving some other object in its place. What actually happens is that the wood rat collects one item and is in the process of carrying it home when it finds something better. It cannot carry both objects, so it drops its original prize in favor of the more desirable one.

Wood rats are careful and discerning architects. Their nests can be huge, up to 5 feet (1.5 m) across and the same in height. They are often built around the base of a spiny cactus. The spines are built into the fabric of the nest so that it is difficult for another animal to get inside. Desert wood rats are experts at moving among the spines and can do so very quickly

⊕ *A desert wood rat in the southwestern United States. The alternative name of "pack rat" refers to the animal's habit of transporting objects around its range.*

without ever seeming to injure themselves. The nest offers a refuge from the extremes of heat and cold typical of the desert climate. It is also impregnable to most predators. The nest may contain several chambers. Some are lined with soft material and used for sleeping, while others serve as larders. A wood rat can build a basic nest in about a week, but often it does not have to start from scratch. Many nests are used time and again by generations of wood rats, each extending or modifying them to their own personal specifications. Some nests are known to be hundreds of years old. Desert wood rats eat all kinds of plant material, but succulent cacti are especially important because they provide moisture as well as food. Desert wood rats rarely get the opportunity to drink free water.

Life is particularly hard for nursing mothers who must also find enough water to convert into milk for their young. The mothers of large litters sometimes die in the effort to sustain their offspring. But as a rule, wood rat litters are fairly small, and females generally produce only two or three litters a year. The young disperse once they are weaned.

Endearing Pets

Adult wood rats live solitary lives, although they are nonaggressive and nonterritorial, and their home ranges overlap with those of their neighbors. They can be tamed if captured when young and make endearing pets. Nonetheless, they can also create a nuisance to farmers and homeowners who do not wish to trade their electrical wiring, nuts and bolts, and even silver jewelry for gifts of twig and bone. However, the animals are rarely numerous enough to be considered a serious pest.

Common name Golden hamster (Syrian hamster)

Scientific name *Mesocricetus auratus*

Family   Muridae

Order   Rodentia

Size   Length head/body: 6.5–7 in (17–18 cm); tail length: 0.5 in (1 cm)

    Weight 3.5–4 oz (99–113 g)

Key features Short-tailed animal with sandy fur fading to white on belly; head broad with prominent rounded ears and huge cheek pouches; females have 12–16 mammae

Habits   Mostly nocturnal; burrowing; socially aggressive; capable of hibernation

Breeding   Three to 5 litters of 2–16 young born at any time of year (mostly spring and summer) after gestation period of 16–19 days. Weaned at 20 days; sexually mature at 8 weeks. May live 3 years in captivity, fewer in the wild

Voice   Generally silent

Diet   Very varied: includes seeds, shoots, fruit, and other plant material; also insects and other invertebrates and meat scavenged as carrion

Habitat   Steppe and dry, rocky, scrubland

Distribution Aleppo region of northwestern Syria

Status   Population: probably a few hundred in the wild; IUCN Endangered. Many thousands bred in captivity every year

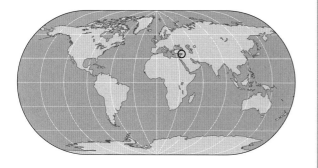

Golden Hamster *Mesocricetus auratus*

The familiar golden hamster is well known and loved as a children's pet, but many of the characteristics that make it so appealing are in fact adaptations to life in the dry, hostile deserts of the Middle East.

WERE IT NOT FOR THE GOLDEN HAMSTER's worldwide popularity as a pet, it would probably not merit a mention here. In the wild it is an unremarkable rodent, and its natural range is restricted to a small part of northwestern Syria. Before the 1930s very few people would have known what a hamster was. They were simply one of the hundreds of mouselike rodents too obscure to have common names.

The First Captives

In 1930 four young golden hamsters were captured, and one of them, the only female, produced a large litter of 12 young. The hamsters proved easy to keep and breed in captivity. Within 10 years they were becoming popular pets and laboratory animals in Britain and the United States. By the early 1970s domestic hamsters were familiar throughout much of the developed world, but every one was a descendant of that single Syrian female—not a healthy state of affairs. In 1971 an expedition was dispatched to Syria to find and collect more wild hamsters. A total of 13 new animals were brought to the United States to improve the bloodline of domestic stock.

Among the hamster's most distinctive features are its huge cheek pouches. They open inside the mouth but stay dry, so they can easily be emptied. The cheek pouches extend well beyond the back of the hamster's head, past its shoulders. When full, the pouches are at least as large as the hamster's skull. Hence they can

be used to carry large quantities of food and bedding material. Hamsters have been known to store many hundreds of times their own body weight in food in underground larders. Mother hamsters even use their pouches to carry their babies to safety if the nest is disturbed. Newborn litters can be transported in one go, with five or more young packed into each pouch.

Antisocial Habits

Wild golden hamsters live in burrows, which they fight to defend. Their chief weapons are their long incisor teeth, which remain sharp through constant use. Hamsters clearly recognize each other individually, probably by smell, but rarely tolerate each other's presence for long. Males and females in estrus suspend hostilities just long enough to mate, then go their separate ways. Most other hamster species are similarly unsociable. Several are even more aggressive, willing to attack almost any other animal that comes too close regardless of size.

Hamster burrows consist of tunnels up to 4 feet (1.2 m) deep, with several chambers used for different purposes, such as sleeping, food storage, and raising young. Females are a little larger than males and have an unusually high number of nipples—often 14, but sometimes as many as 16. Litters of baby hamsters develop amazingly quickly. They are born blind, naked, and helpless, but at three weeks old they look like smaller versions of their parents and are able to look after themselves.

Young hamsters can breed when they are barely two months old. Meanwhile, their mother may have already raised another family! Populations can therefore build up rapidly and include many generations of hamsters. A few that escaped from an English pet shop quickly became a population of several hundred and damaged local footpaths by their burrowing.

⊕ *The cute, furry looks of the golden hamster are deceptive—the animals will fight viciously to defend their burrows and will only tolerate each other's presence for a brief time in the breeding season.*

Common name
Mongolian gerbil (Mongolian jird)

Scientific name
Meriones unguiculatus

Family	Muridae
Order	Rodentia
Size	Length head/body: 4–7 in (10–18 cm); tail length: 4–7 in (10–18 cm)
Weight	1.4–2.5 oz (40–71 g)
Key features	Small, sand-colored rodent; long, furry tail with brushy tip; hind feet long, all toes bear long claws; ears small but prominent
Habits	Lives alone or in family groups; active day and night and all year round; sleeps and stores food in burrows
Breeding	Up to 3 litters of 1–12 (usually 4–7) young born in spring, summer, or fall after gestation period of 19–21 days. Weaned at 3 weeks; sexually mature at 15 weeks. May live several years in captivity, rarely more than 2 in the wild
Voice	Various squeaking sounds; also signals by drumming feet on ground
Diet	All kinds of plant material, including seeds, shoots, roots, and fruit; also insects
Habitat	Desert
Distribution	Mongolia, southern Siberia, and northern Chinese provinces of Sinkiang and Manchuria
Status	Population: abundant

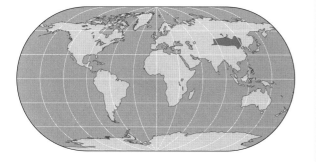

RODENTS

Mongolian Gerbil

Meriones unguiculatus

Gerbils (more correctly known as jirds) are the Old World equivalent of small American desert rodents, such as kangaroo mice. The gerbil family includes some of the best-adapted desert animals.

GERBILS HAVE LONG, SOFT, slightly grizzled fur, usually close in color to the sand in which they live. The Mongolian gerbil, which is adapted to life in the stony deserts of eastern-central Asia, has a white belly and feet and rich golden fur on its back, flanks, and head. The longer hairs along its back are tipped with black or gray. The tip of the tail is dark, like a soft, worn-out artist's paintbrush. The coat provides good camouflage, and the dark tail tip may act as a decoy, distracting attention away from the gerbil's head in the event of an attack. Gerbil ears are extremely sensitive and can hear sounds well outside the range of human hearing. At the slightest sign of danger the animals leap off with astounding speed and disappear into a secure burrow.

Living with Extremes

Gerbils are hardy animals. They remain active all year round, enduring extremes of temperature from freezing winters to blazing-hot summers. They also have to contend with a year-round shortage of water. Mongolian jirds live in relatively simple, shallow burrows, with two or three "rooms." One such room is used for sleeping and is furnished with a bed of dry grass and vegetation; other chambers nearer the entrance are used as larders. They may contain as much as 40 pounds (18 kg) of stored food, usually nonperishable seeds and grains.

Mongolian gerbils are among the most social jirds. Several males and females often live together in a burrow, along with young of

Mongolian jirds live in mixed-sex groups that dwell in a communal burrow. The animals collectively hoard food for winter and huddle together during the coldest months.

various ages. The adult males appear to help with grooming and keeping the young warm. However, in captivity they are often removed in the belief that their ministrations do more harm than good, distracting the mother and preventing her suckling as much as the family needs. More recent research suggests that in the wild the adults living together in a burrow are more likely to be siblings than mated pairs. Estrous females leave the burrow to mate with unrelated males living nearby, then return to the home burrow to rear their litter. The males observed tending young gerbils in the wild may in fact be the uncle rather than the father.

Farmer's Foe

Mongolian jirds are extremely active and may wander 1 mile (1.6 km) each day in search of food. Young animals can disperse 20 miles (32 km) or more over a period of time. As a result, the species readily colonizes new areas where a suitable food source becomes available. People farming land on the edge of the desert therefore regard gerbils as pests and hunt them with dogs or gas their burrows in an attempt to control them. Elsewhere the species is more popular. It has been a popular children's pet since the 1950s and is also used fairly extensively as a laboratory animal.

The Mongolian gerbil is just one of nearly 100 species in the gerbil family, many of which are similar in appearance. Several are officially listed by the IUCN as Endangered, being restricted to small patches of habitat that are threatened by agricultural development or climate change.

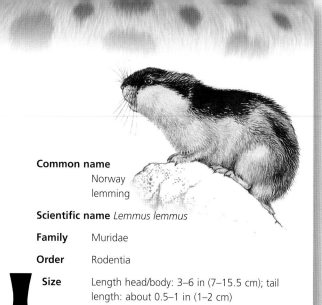

Common name
Norway lemming

Scientific name *Lemmus lemmus*

Family Muridae

Order Rodentia

Size Length head/body: 3–6 in (7–15.5 cm); tail length: about 0.5–1 in (1–2 cm)

Weight 0.4–5 oz (11–142 g)

Key features Rounded body and head; very short tail; thick coat is creamy-yellow on underside, legs, and feet, but deep reddish-brown on back; darker still on shoulders, head, and face; ears small and hidden in fur; eyes small and bright; thumb of each front foot bears large, flat snow claw

Habits Active at any time of day; does not hibernate; lives in burrows in ground or snow; swims well; aggressive and unsociable; overcrowded populations occasionally undertake mass migrations

Breeding Up to 6 litters of 1–13 (usually 5–8) young born in spring and summer (or every 21 days all year round under ideal conditions) after gestation period of 16–23 days. Weaned at 14–16 days; females sexually mature at 2–3 weeks, males at 3–4 weeks. May live up to 2 years, usually fewer, in the wild; not normally kept in captivity

Voice Various squeaks and whistles

Diet Mostly mosses; also leaves and shoots of grasses and sedges, lichen, fruit, and bark

Habitat Tundra

Distribution Norway, Sweden, Finland, and extreme northwestern Russia

Status Population: generally abundant but fluctuates wildly from year to year

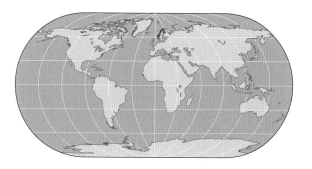

Norway Lemming

Lemmus lemmus

Legend has it that when the going gets tough, Norway lemmings commit mass suicide, leaping straight over the nearest cliff. In fact, lemmings are as well versed in the art of self-preservation as any other wild animal, so what drives them to such recklessness?

LEMMINGS ENDURE SOME OF the harshest living conditions of any small mammal. In winter the sun dips below the horizon for three months at a time, the tundra is blanketed in snow, and air temperatures plummet to -86°F (-30°C) or lower. But lemmings do not hibernate, nor do they store food to see them through the winter. Instead, they adopt a hidden life under the snow, remaining active and foraging even on the very coldest days.

Arctic Survival

Each lemming builds a snug nest of dry grass, lichen, and leaves on the surface of the frozen ground, but beneath 36 to 48 inches (91 to 122 cm) of snow. Tunnels radiate out from the nest, and the lemming moves around them quite freely, seeking the green growth of mosses and other tundra plants. Its coat is thick and warm, and the ears and tail are small, reducing the risk of frostbite. The first toe on each front foot bears a large, spade-shaped claw ideal for shoveling snow. Only in summer, when the snow has gone, do lemmings dig into the ground itself. The summer burrows are shallow because below 12 to 24 inches (30 to 61 cm) of soil the ground remains permanently frozen all year round. Summer nests therefore have to be just as well insulated as winter ones: If there is a sudden thaw, burrows may flood or collapse as the ground turns to a chilly mush.

Lemmings breed exceptionally fast, even by rodent standards. Females bear large litters in quick succession, and young lemmings are

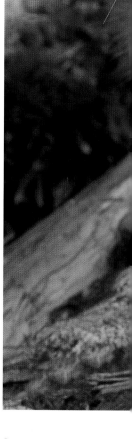

⊕ *The significance of lemmings in their arctic environment is second only to humans. They are the main prey of several predators, and their tunnels help loosen and defrost top layers of soil so that plants can grow.*

themselves able to breed very early. Females can conceive when they are only two weeks old. Normally, breeding is restricted to the warmer summer months, and productivity is matched by high rates of mortality. However, every two to five years a combination of mild weather and plentiful food means that breeding also happens in the winter. Lemming numbers start to multiply early, vastly increasing the rate the population grows in the spring. Population densities in "lemming years" can increase over a hundredfold, up to 4,000 per acre (10,000 per ha).

Driven to Despair

Lemmings are not sociable creatures. They are highly aggressive and appear to detest other members of their species. So in lemming years, when space becomes scarce, youngsters are forced to disperse by the thousand. The young probably set out alone, but soon find themselves in the company of many others, all heading the same way. Lemming migrations can be so sudden that Scandinavian people once believed the animals must have rained down from the sky. The abnormal behavior may be partly due to mild poisoning, when lack of food forces the animals to feed on unsuitable plants. Traveling in large crowds is highly stressful for such solitary animals, yet hordes of demented lemmings careering over cliffs and into rivers are certainly not deliberate mass suicides. Ironically, it is exactly the opposite: It is the lemmings' powerful urge to survive by getting away from others of the species that leads to panic and ends in disaster for many.

⬅ *Norway lemmings are unsociable, intolerant creatures: Every two to five years their numbers rise dramatically—an increase in aggressive behavior results from this population surge. In the conflict shown here, two males adopt threatening postures toward one another (1), box (2), and wrestle (3).*

Common name Field vole (short-tailed vole)

Scientific name *Microtus agrestis*

Family	Muridae
Order	Rodentia
Size	Length head/body: 3–5 in (8–13 cm); tail length: 1–2 in (2–5 cm)

Weight 0.5–1.8 oz (14–50 g)

Key features	Round bodied and short nosed, with short pinkish tail; fur uniformly gray-brown above, paler on belly; ears short, often hidden by fur
Habits	Mostly nocturnal and crepuscular; territorial and aggressive; digs burrows and also creates runways in grass
Breeding	Up to 7 litters of 1–12 young (usually 4–6) born spring to fall after gestation period of 19–25 days. Weaned at 2 weeks; females sexually mature at 4 weeks, males at 6 weeks. May live up to 2 years in captivity, usually fewer in the wild
Voice	Loud squeaks; chirps and chattering noises when angry
Diet	Herbivorous: mostly grass; also leaves, shoots, and bark of other plants
Habitat	Grassland: common in lightly grazed pasture and field edges with longish grass; also heaths and moorland
Distribution	Throughout northern Europe, including Scandinavia and Britain (but not Ireland); east to central Siberia
Status	Population: abundant, probably hundreds of millions

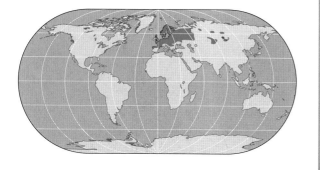

Field Vole

Microtus agrestis

The European field vole is one of the most common and widespread members of the genus Microtus, *the small-eared voles. At the last count the genus was thought to include 65 distinct species from all over the Northern Hemisphere.*

FIELD VOLES ARE TOUGH LITTLE animals, with a fat body and a grizzled gray-brown coat. They molt their fur twice a year, and the winter coat has an extrathick underlayer of fine hairs that form a dense felt. The coat is longer and thicker in northern field voles, which tend to be larger than their southern relatives. Field voles are active all year round and spend most of their waking hours collecting food.

"Grass Vole"

As their name suggests, field voles live in grassy areas, preferring long tussocky stems that provide plenty of shelter as well as food. The average field vole needs to eat approximately its own body weight in grass each day to sustain itself. Grass stems and leaves are a tough diet, and the field vole's molar teeth are endowed with many elaborate cusps and sharp edges to help grind the food. Such features are much more pronounced than in similar voles with softer diets of fruit, fungi, and succulent stems. In fact, the field vole might be better named "grass vole," since it lives in grass, eats grass, and makes its nest of grass.

Because grass is easy to find, field voles never need to wander far from their burrows to forage. Some females spend their entire adult lives in an area of fewer than 1,100 square feet (100 sq. m), about the size of a tennis court. Females are generally nonterritorial except when rearing young. Males, on the other hand, are highly aggressive and will fight viciously to maintain a territory up to 10 times bigger than that of the average female range. Owning a large territory is desirable, since it gives the resident male access to several females.

four weeks, sometimes giving birth to 40 or more young in one exhausting season.

Not surprisingly, with such prolific breeding capabilities vole numbers can sometimes build up quickly. There are several well-documented cases of vole plagues. However, such population explosions are fairly unusual, simply because in most years the vole death rate is easily high enough to balance out the births.

Keystone Species

Being fat, relatively slow moving, and confined to areas of open grassland, the field vole is at the top of the menu for an extraordinarily long list of predators. They include commonplace animals such as foxes, kestrels, and badgers, and also many threatened ones, including wildcats, pine martens, polecats, eagles, and barn owls. Breeding success and survival in many of these species is directly linked to vole numbers. The field vole is therefore a good example of a keystone species without which many others would collapse. It is in need of protection in countries where natural grassland is under threat from farming and development.

⬆ A field vole stands on a moss-covered log. The animals are active at all times of year, normally hidden among dense, tussocky grass.

Scent is important to field voles. Mature males in particular have large scent glands on their hips, which spread scent all over their territory as they brush against grass stems. Female voles are induced ovulators, which means they do not come into breeding condition until a suitable male is present. The mere scent of a sexually active male is enough to bring an adult female into estrus and to accelerate the development of juvenile females. Female voles mature quickly and are capable of conceiving at just four weeks. From then on they can rear a litter of young every three or

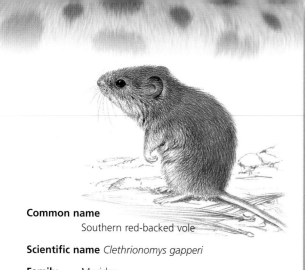

Common name
Southern red-backed vole

Scientific name *Clethrionomys gapperi*

Family   Muridae

Order   Rodentia

Size   Length head/body: 3–5 in (8–13 cm); tail length: 1–2 in (3–5 cm)

Weight 0.2–1.5 oz (6–43 g)

Key features Rounded body with short legs; tail about half length of body; fur grayish-brown with redddish flush along back; face short with prominent black eyes and large, rounded ears

Habits   Active day and night and all year round; territorial; climbs well

Breeding   Up to 4 litters of 1–11 young (litters larger in north) born early spring to fall after gestation period of 17–20 days. Weaned at 3 weeks; sexually mature at 3 months. May live over 4 years in captivity, up to 20 months in the wild

Voice   Soft, chirping alarm call and audible clattering of teeth

Diet   Fruit, nuts, fungi, lichen, green shoots, and other vegetation; also insects

Habitat   Tundra, moorland, mossy forest undergrowth, and woodland floors

Distribution Southern Canada from British Columbia to Newfoundland; northern coterminous U.S. south to Arizona

Status   Population: abundant

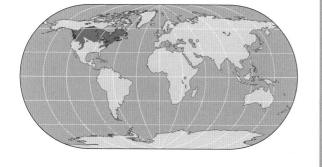

Southern Red-Backed Vole
Clethrionomys gapperi

The southern red-backed vole is typical of the widespread genus Clethrionomys. *Similar voles occupy much the same kind of habitat in other parts of North America and in Europe and Asia.*

AS A GENERAL RULE, MEMBERS OF the vole branch of the mouse family—which includes the lemmings—are creatures of high northern latitudes. Their chubby bodies, short legs and tail, and small, neat ears are adaptations to a cool climate, since they reduce the surface area through which body warmth can escape.

Chestnut-Red Stripe

Red-backed voles are ideally suited to life in cool, damp climates such as the Canadian tundra and boreal forest. Farther south suitable habitat is restricted to the mountains of the Rockies and Appalachians. The southern red-backed vole characteristically has a thick coat of muted gray-brown fur, typically highlighted with a broad stripe of rich chestnut-red running from head to tail down the animal's back.

Southern red-backed voles are opportunist feeders, and their diet tends to reflect seasonal availability. In spring they eat mostly green shoots and tender new leaves, while in summer energy-rich fruits take precedence. Later they take advantage of seeds and nuts, storing any they cannot eat to help see them through the lean times ahead. The vole's teeth, including its grinding molars, continue to grow well into adult life. When the molars eventually stop growing and form roots, the vole's days are numbered, since the teeth become worn out by munching on tough vegetable matter. Once they stop working properly, the vole will starve. But few voles survive long enough for their teeth to let them down. Most die of other causes at an earlier age. The voles are preyed on by a wide variety of mammals and birds.

The reddish coat distinguishes this group of species from other voles. Unlike mice, typical voles have a snub-nosed appearance and ears that do not project far out of the fur.

Except for females with young, red-backed voles live alone in well-spaced home ranges, which vary in size depending on sex, habitat quality, and season. Winter territories are small, as little as half an acre (0.2 ha), because snow restricts the voles' movement. In summer the voles may occupy ranges 10 times as large. It is a considerable area for such a small animal, but the voles are quite fiercely territorial. They will drive out intruders, including animals of other species. Scent markers play an important part in staking out territories, as does sound.

The voles utter sharp chirping calls to advertise their presence to other voles. If the resident vole is killed, its territory will not remain vacant for long. When moving around their territory, red-backed voles tend to bound along open routes. They use fallen logs or runways created by the regular movements of other larger animals, but they do not stray far from cover. Red-backed voles remain active during the winter, creating personal networks of tunnels under the snow from which they can forage for fungi, lichen, and tree bark.

Starting Early

Young red-backed voles are able to breed at the age of three months, but young born late in the summer may have to wait until the following year before making their first attempt. The breeding season starts surprisingly early, often in late winter, when there is still a covering of snow on the ground. However, if a female is in good condition, there is no reason why she cannot rear a healthy litter, which will be ready to emerge as soon as the snow melts away. The young of that litter will themselves be breeding within a few weeks.

Common name
Muskrat

Scientific name *Ondatra zibethicus*

Family Muridae

Order Rodentia

Size Length head/body: 9–13 in (23–33 cm); tail length: 7–11.5 in (18–29 cm)

Weight 1.5–4 lb (0.6–1.8 kg)

Key features Huge brown or black rat with glossy fur and large, partially webbed hind feet; tail naked and slightly flattened from side to side

Habits Mostly nocturnal and crepuscular; social but bad tempered; semiaquatic

Breeding Up to 6 litters of 1–11 young born at any time of year (spring and summer in north of range) after gestation period of 25–30 days. Weaned at 2–3 weeks; sexually mature at 6–8 weeks in south of range, later in north. May live up to 10 years in captivity, rarely more than 3 in the wild

Voice Growls when annoyed

Diet Mostly aquatic plants such as reeds, rushes, cattails, and water lilies; also grasses and animal matter, including fish and shellfish

Habitat Pools, lakes, rivers, marshes, and swamps with plenty of plant life

Distribution Southern Canada and most of U.S.; patchy in California and Texas; introduced in Eurasia and South America; introduced British population exterminated within a few years

Status Population: abundant—many thousands, perhaps millions. Trapped for fur and meat; considered a pest in parts of introduced range in Europe

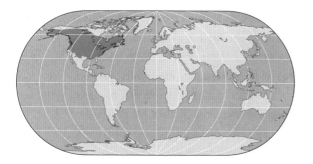

Muskrat

Ondatra zibethicus

The muskrat is not really a rat at all, but a kind of large vole. Its native home is North America, but thanks to a little help from humans it now also occupies huge areas of mainland Europe and Asia.

COMMON MUSKRATS ARE LARGE rodents that feed mostly on water plants, which they gather beneath the surface of still- and slow-flowing rivers and lakes. Anatomical clues to their semiaquatic lifestyle include a tail that is flattened from side to side for use as a rudder and partially webbed hind feet. The feet also bear a fringe of stiff hairs on the outer edges, which act a bit like fins. The hairs increase the surface area the muskrat can use to paddle through the water. They may also help grip slippery floating logs and perhaps stop the animal from sinking in soft mud. Muskrats are superb swimmers and divers. If need be, they can remain submerged for over a quarter of an hour, although most dives are much shorter— about three minutes on average.

Muskrat Architecture

Depending on their habitat, muskrats live either in waterside burrows or in houses built of plant stems and mud. Burrows are dug directly into the banks of rivers. They are difficult to see because the entrances are well below the water level. The reason for positioning the entrances so far down is to ensure that they are not exposed during low water or frozen over in the winter. Shallow water that freezes from top to bottom in winter is not suitable for muskrats.

Where there is no bank, in areas of marshland, for example, the muskrats build one of their own by collecting large quantities of plant material into a heap and covering it with a thick layer of mud. The mound rots down into a dense mass within which the muskrat creates a nesting chamber above the water line. Like burrows in a natural bank, the "houses" are accessible only from below.

SEE ALSO Bear, American Black **2**:90; Vole, Water **7**:98

In the far north of the muskrat's range, where pools and rivers are frozen over for much of the winter, the muskrat also builds temporary shelters over holes in the ice. These "tents" provide the muskrat with a secluded spot in which to feed and rest between foraging dives.

Muskrats live alone or in family groups, members of which help defend territory and build and maintain the houses if necessary. While suckling a litter of babies, the female excludes her mate from the breeding nest, forcing him to live in a nearby burrow or a separate nest attached to the main house. Muskrats are potentially prolific breeders, but litter sizes vary geographically. In the south litters are small, but there can be as many as six in a season. In the north families are larger, but there are fewer litters per year.

Muskrats are well adapted to a life in and around water. They have partially webbed hind feet and a flattened tail, which they use as a rudder. Here muskrats feed on aquatic plants.

In the last hundred years muskrats have been intensively hunted and trapped for their glossy, luxurient fur. At its peak in the early 1970s the North American fur trade marketed over 10 million muskrat skins a year, worth more than $40 million. Demand for fur has since declined, but the muskrat is still an economically important animal.

Widespread Aliens

It was their status as fur-bearers that encouraged humans to introduce muskrats to several places outside their natural range, and the species is now a widespread alien in Europe, Asia, and South America. Muskrats were introduced to fur farms in Britain between 1927 and 1932. Many escaped and soon spread widely. Over 4,500 were trapped, and the species was eliminated by 1937. Elsewhere, some populations now support a profitable fur trade, while others have caused significant damage to wetland ecosystems. Muskrats are especially unpopular in the Netherlands. Here their burrowing and feeding activities threaten to destabilize the dikes that protect large areas of reclaimed agricultural land from flooding.

Common name Water vole (north European water vole, water rat)

Scientific name *Arvicola terrestris*

Family	Muridae
Order	Rodentia
Size	Length head/body: 5–9 in (12–23 cm); tail length: 1.5–5.5 in (4–14 cm). Northern animals larger than those in south

Weight 3–11 oz (85–312 g)

Key features	Chubby, ratlike rodent with rounded head and body, blunt face, and thin, hairy tail; rich glossy brown fur that grows quite long
Habits	Semiaquatic; solitary; active day and night and all year round
Breeding	Two to 5 litters of 2–8 (usually 4–6 young) born between spring and fall after gestation period of 20–22 days. Weaned at 2–3 weeks; sexually mature at 1–12 months (British voles only breed after their first winter). May live up to 5 years in captivity, rarely more than 18 months in the wild
Voice	Usually silent; may give harsh clicking call when alarmed; squeaks when angry
Diet	Grasses, sedges, and roots; occasionally catches and eats fish
Habitat	Banks of slow-flowing streams and rivers; also away from water in meadows and pastures
Distribution	Widespread throughout most of Europe east through Siberia to Mongolia; absent from Iceland, Ireland, much of France, Spain, and Portugal; patchy distribution in Greece
Status	Population: abundant, many thousands. Dramatic recent decline of British population threatens species with extinction there

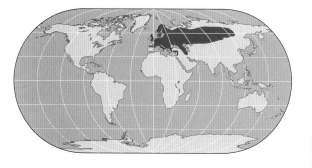

Water Vole

Arvicola terrestris

Immortalized as "Ratty," the wise and loyal water rat in Kenneth Grahame's classic children's book The Wind in the Willows, *this endearing character of the riverbank is really not a rat at all.*

RATTY WAS A PARTICULARLY British water vole, because if there was one thing he loved more than anything else, it was his quiet riverbank home. In eastern Europe and Siberia, however, water voles are often found living in fields and grasslands, well away from rivers. Here they spend much of their lives underground, constructing extensive burrow systems. They feed on roots and bulbs, and sometimes cause significant damage to crops with their burrowing. Such variability in habitat partly explains the contradiction between the water vole's common and scientific names—*terrestris* means "earth-dweller."

Riverside Homes

Riverbank voles burrow, too. Their nests are constructed in a chamber well above the water, but there is usually at least one submerged entrance. Other entrances are often hidden by tussocky vegetation. During the breeding season female voles block their tunnel openings with grass to keep nosey neighbors out and wandering babies in.

Voles are territorial during the breeding season, which can last as long as eight months in mild years. Male territories stretch along about 330 to 660 feet (100 to 200 m) of water's edge. They overlap with those of females, which are roughly half the size. Neither males nor females will tolerate an adult of the same sex intruding on their patch, and fights are common. To avoid disputes, water voles will mark out their territory by leaving piles of feces

 SEE ALSO Mink, American **1**:52; Vole, Field **7**:92; Muskrat **7**:96

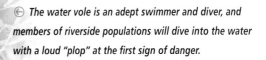

⊖ *The water vole is an adept swimmer and diver, and members of riverside populations will dive into the water with a loud "plop" at the first sign of danger.*

voles do not hibernate, but store away quantities of clipped grass and other food so they can afford to stay indoors during periods of bad weather. Otherwise they continue to forage all through the winter months, switching from green shoots to roots, bulbs, and the bark of trees such as alder and willow. Such food can be reached even when the ground is frozen or covered in snow.

The water vole is the largest native European member of the vole subfamily (Microtinae). It is equivalent in many ways to the North American muskrat, although it is less fully adapted to a life in water. For example, its hind feet bear a short swimming fringe, but there is no webbing between the toes. In the water voles are safe from most predators except the notorious mink. As well as being able to catch voles while they are swimming, the mink is small enough to enter vole burrows.

Mink and Other Dangers

The arrival of the American mink in Europe, especially in Britain, has been bad news for water voles. The mink, which were originally imported to stock fur farms, have become well established in the wild. Here they have had a serious effect on native wildlife, including voles and waterbirds. But the mink is just one of a number of factors contributing to a steep but steady decline in British water vole numbers.

Straightening of rivers and "tidying up" overgrown banks, as well as cultivation of crops right up to the water's edge, have each played a part in reducing water vole numbers. Water pollution and other disturbances further threaten the species. Many parts of Britain have lost over 90 percent of their water voles since 1990, making them Britain's fastest declining mammal. The spread of alien mink in Europe may soon threaten the vole there, too.

at the water's edge. The latrines convey scent messages to other voles and are a highly typical sign of the vole's presence, along with its little four-fingered prints in the soft mud. The fecal pellets are often bright green as a result of feeding on aquatic plants. During the winter, however, relationships tend to be more amicable. Often several adults will share a single burrow, huddling in a large nest for warmth. Water

1946961

Common name Lesser blind mole rat (Balkan blind mole rat)

Scientific name *Nannospalax leucodon* (formerly *Spalax leucodon*)

Family Muridae

Order Rodentia

Size Length head/body: 6–11 in (15–27 cm)

Weight 3.5–7.5 oz (100–213 g)

Key features Long body with short legs and large, clawed feet; no visible tail, eyes, or ears; face dominated by large nose and huge protruding incisor teeth; light-brown fur with prominent white facial stripe

Habits Active day and night; burrowing: hardly ever emerges at surface; solitary and territorial

Breeding Litters of 1–5 (usually 2–4) young born January–April after gestation period of 1 month. Weaned at 3–4 weeks; probably sexually mature at about 2–3 months. May live up to 4.5 years, usually many fewer in the wild, not normally kept in captivity

Voice Generally silent, but appears to signal by drumming head on roof of tunnels

Diet Roots and tubers, including crops such as potatoes; also acorns and plant stems

Habitat Well-drained soils under wooded or open ground

Distribution Balkan peninsula, Romania, and Bulgaria

Status Population: not known, probably several thousand; IUCN Vulnerable. Increasingly rare and patchy in distribution

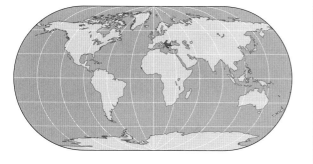

Lesser Blind Mole Rat

Nannospalax leucodon

Sightless and antisocial, the blind mole rats of southeastern Europe live alone underground in elaborate, self-excavated labyrinths. Unlike true moles, however, they are strict vegetarians.

THERE ARE MANY DIFFERENT kinds of burrowing rodent, but none is more wholly adapted to life underground than the blind mole rats. The lesser blind mole rat is one of the better-known species owing to its unfortunate habit of raiding root crops such as potatoes and beets. The culprits remain unseen, since they rarely emerge above ground, preferring to whip the vegetables away surreptitiously from below. But their guilty secret is betrayed by large stockpiles of stolen crops stashed away in underground larders. Unfortunately, the species has declined greatly as a result of land development and direct persecution by farmers.

Blind Burrowers

The blind mole rat has no eyes and no visible ears. The latter are hidden deep in the animal's dense fur to prevent them from getting clogged with dirt. External ear flaps would soon be torn or damaged as the mole rat moved along its tight tunnels. Sight and hearing aside, the mole rat's other senses are acute. The face has stiff sensory bristles, and the large nose is covered in tough skin so that it can be shoved roughly into tightly packed soil to sniff out food.

Mole rat burrows are impressive structures. Those of the closely related Balkan blind mole rat can have anything up to 640 feet (195 m) of tunnels. The tunnels themselves are between 6 inches (15 cm) and 13 feet (4 m) deep and link dozens of rooms. The deepest tunnels tend to be built and used only during periods of very cold or very dry weather. The shallow tunnels, which extend among the roots of plants, are used for foraging. The tunnels and animals

inside them are vulnerable to farm machinery, especially tractor-drawn plows. Since mole rats are not used to dispersing over long distances, they have no way of escaping the destruction of their habitat by development. As a result, the animals are becoming rare.

Roof Drumming

Except for mothers with young, blind mole rats live alone in their burrows and are fiercely territorial. They communicate by drumming their head against the roof and walls of the tunnels; the sound vibrations travel through the ground to the burrows of other mole rats.

Females prepare for the breeding season by constructing large mounds of compacted soil at the surface. The mounds are riddled with tunnels and contain at their center a grass-lined nesting chamber. There are also several smaller chambers for storage and toilets. The mounds can be several feet (approximately 1 m) in diameter and up to 24 inches (61 cm) high. The largest ones are built in wet areas, where burrows are in danger of flooding. The mound ensures the babies remain high and dry during any spring floods.

The breeding mound is usually surrounded by an encampment of smaller mounds that are built by adult male mole rats in an attempt to court the female. The male announces his presence by drumming on the roof before attempting to tunnel into her burrow system to mate. Unwelcome suitors are aggressively repelled, and the male mole rat plays no part in rearing his young.

ⓓ *Unlike the true moles, which use their "hands" for digging, mole rats burrow using their teeth. Like beavers, a mole rat's lips can close behind the teeth to prevent dirt from getting into the mouth.*

The Dormouse Family

Dormice look like miniature squirrels and occupy an ecological niche part way between those of true mice and squirrels. Their eyes are large to suit their nocturnal habits, and their feet are adapted for climbing. There are four fingers on the front feet and five toes on the back, all of which have short, sharp claws that can hook into rough surfaces such as tree bark. In the absence of a thumb dormice have raised, flexible pads on the palms of their front feet, which help grip branches. The pads secrete a sticky substance that enables the dormice to climb even very smooth surfaces.

Dormice spend most of their active time off the ground, up among the branches of trees and shrubs. However, some species, like garden and forest dormice, spend at least some time foraging for insects and other invertebrates on the ground. The desert dormouse is an

⊕ *The Japanese dormouse is classified by the IUCN as Endangered. Elsewhere, other dormouse species, such as the edible dormouse, are also at risk.*

entirely terrestrial species that lives in burrows and sheltered spaces under fallen logs or in heaps of fallen leaves.

The furry tail of the dormouse acts as a counterbalance when climbing and as a snug wraparound blanket when sleeping. The tail skin of several species comes off easily if grabbed by a predator. This may allow the dormouse to escape, but the remains of its tail dry up and break off, leaving the animal tailless. Dormice seem to manage quite well without a tail, and animals with all or part of their tails missing are quite common.

Origins

The dormouse family is an ancient one. Fossil evidence suggests that the group first appeared in Europe in the mid-Eocene period about 45 million years ago. From there they spread to Africa and Asia. In the Pleistocene period several Mediterranean islands supported populations of giant dormice. While little can be deduced about the lifestyle and behavior of those animals, preserved remains show that they were remarkably similar to the common dormice of today, except that they were about three times their size.

Family Gliridae: 3 subfamilies, 8 genera, 26 species

Subfamily Graphiurinae (African dormice): 1 genus, 14 species

  Graphiurus includes spectacled dormouse (*G. ocularis*)

Subfamily Leithiinae (forest, garden, desert, and mouse-tailed dormice): 4 genera, 9 species

  Dryomys 3 species, woolly dormouse (*D. laniger*); forest dormouse (*D. nitedula*); Chinese dormouse (*D. sichuanensis*)

  Eliomys 2 species, Asiatic garden dormouse (*E. melanurus*); garden dormouse (*E. quercinus*)

  Myomimus 3 species, masked mouse-tailed dormouse (*M. personatus*); Roach's mouse-tailed dormouse (*M. roachi*); Setzer's mouse-tailed dormouse (*M. setzeri*)

  Selvinia 1 species, desert dormouse (*S. betpakdalaensis*)

Subfamily Glirinae 3 genera, 3 species

  Glirulus 1 species, Japanese dormouse (*G. japonicus*)

  Muscardinus 1 species, hazel dormouse (*M. avellanarius*)

  Glis 1 species, edible dormouse (*G. glis*)

 SEE ALSO Squirrel Family, The **7**:34; Mouse and Rat Family, The **7**:64

⊕ The garden dormouse has distinctive black markings around the eyes. It is widespread in Europe, occupying a range of habitats from sand dunes to woodlands and rocky mountain slopes.

in which they must live entirely off their stored fat reserves.

Leaves may not be much use to dormice as food, but they are nonetheless useful as building materials and often incorporated into nests. Nests are roughly spherical and are used in summer for sleeping and rearing young.

Individual adult African dormice occupy home ranges of up to 30 acres (12 ha), while hazel dormice rarely venture more than 200 feet (60 m) from home. Most dormice are social to some extent and will share nests with other animals, often family members. Breeding females may be territorial, and males will fight for dominance at the start of the mating season. Dormice are among the noisier small rodents and use a wide variety of clicking, whistling, and churring calls to communicate with one another.

Lifestyle

The compound cellulose is a complex form of carbohydrate that forms the main structural component of plant leaves. Cellulose offers a valuable source of energy to animals that can digest it. Most rodents have an enlarged cecum—the part of the gut corresponding to the human appendix—that performs the task. Dormice, however, lack a cecum and so cannot properly digest leaves. Instead, they are dependent on a diet of easily digestible sugars and protein, which can be found in fruit, nuts, sap, pollen, and animal matter. Such foods are often markedly seasonal, and dormice tend to specialize in different foods at different times of year. Feeding restrictions are one reason why dormice tend not to breed as fast or live in such high numbers as other mouselike rodents. In winter suitable food is in short supply—the main reason for the prolonged hibernation seen in temperate dormouse species. Dormice gorge themselves on energy-rich foods during summer and fall. Their feasting helps them survive a period of up to nine months

Unusual Dormice

The desert dormouse of Kazakhstan is the subject of much speculation and is sometimes placed in a family of its own. It is an extraordinary-looking animal, especially when fully fattened for hibernation, when its head almost disappears into its round, fat body. Strangely for a desert animal, the desert dormouse is highly susceptible to sunburn. It avoids exposure to bright sunlight by confining its activity to the twilight hours of dusk and dawn. The annual molt is unusual, too, since the desert dormouse sheds several layers of skin along with its hairs.

Another group, known as the Oriental dormice, are not dormice at all but members of the true mouse family, Muridae. Two species are known, the spiny dormouse and the Chinese pygmy dormouse, but both are poorly studied, and little is known of their biology.

103

Common name Edible dormouse
(fat dormouse, glis)

Scientific name *Glis glis*

Family   Gliridae

Order   Rodentia

Size   Length head/body: 5–7.5 in (13–19 cm); tail
length: 4.5–6 in (11–15 cm)

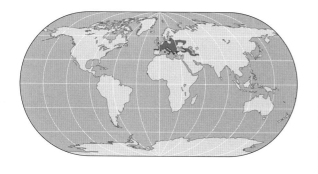

Weight 2.5–6.5 oz (70–184 g)

Key features Squirrel-like animal with silvery gray fur and
darker facial markings; tail gray or brown,
long and bushy

Habits   Nocturnal; arboreal; hibernates for 6–8
months of the year

Breeding   Single (occasionally 2) litters of 2–10 young
born in summer after gestation period of
20–30 days. Weaned at 4 weeks; sexually
mature at about 11 months. May live up to 9
years in captivity, at least 6 in the wild

Voice   Loud whistles and churring calls

Diet   Seeds, fruit, nuts, tree bark, and sap;
occasionally insects, birds' eggs, and nestlings

Habitat   Mature high-canopy woodland, especially
where there are beech trees

Distribution Mainland Europe and Middle East;
introduced to Britain

Status   Population: fairly abundant; IUCN Lower Risk:
near threatened. Considered a pest in much
of Europe, where it is trapped in large
numbers

Edible Dormouse

Glis glis

*The edible dormouse is often referred to by its
scientific name of* glis. *However, it also has a variety
of other names, many of which give clues to
some of its more interesting characteristics.*

IN GERMANY THE EDIBLE DORMOUSE is known as the
Siebenschlafer, meaning "seven-sleeper." The
name has arisen because the animal habitually
hibernates for seven (sometimes eight) months
of the year. The species is also known as the fat
dormouse because it spends the summer
putting on as much weight as possible in order
to survive the long winter. Edible dormice
therefore have a reputation for being greedy.

The natural fattening process was exploited
by the Romans. They kept glis in clay jars,
where they were fed to their heart's content
until they became very fat. They were then
eaten as a delicacy, hence the name "edible"
dormouse. The dormice are still eaten by some
people in Croatia, Slovenia, and southern Italy.
However, they are less popular than formerly,
perhaps because of the effort involved in
catching and rearing them. Even a very fat
individual is too small to make a meal by itself.

Housebreakers

Edible dormice have also been called many rude
names in several languages thanks to their habit
of entering houses and attics. There they do all
kinds of damage, from nibbling stored foods to
gnawing wires. Sometimes they simply run
around in the roof space at night, calling loudly
and keeping the human occupants awake.

In summer edible dormice are tree dwellers.
However, they hibernate in nests on or beneath
the ground, where they are vulnerable to all
kinds of predators. But the risk is worth taking,
because down low there are fewer strong
winds, and temperatures fluctuate less than in
the exposed branches of trees. Deep in a

↑ *Like common dormice, glis are nocturnal. They spend the summer nesting in trees and scrambling nimbly in the branches. Pads on the soles of their feet give a good grip when climbing.*

differences. Edible dormice are about half the size of an adult gray squirrel, with a fatter body and smaller feet. The tail is long and thin and trails the animal, rather than being held erect. The tail is plain brown or gray, and the hairs lack a white fringe. Another special feature is the dark markings that resemble spectacles around the dormouse's eyes. Edible dormice can climb along even the finest branches or scramble among trailing vines in a way the heavier squirrel could never manage.

Major Menace

The preferred habitat of the edible dormouse is tall woodland with plenty of mature nut-bearing trees such as beech. But the dormice make enemies of foresters and horticulturalists by damaging trees. They are a major menace in the almond orchards of Italy, for example. Not only do they ruin crops by devouring the flower buds and eating unripe fruit and nuts, but they also strip the bark from many tree species, destroying vital tissues beneath and sometimes killing the tree from that point up.

Edible dormice are sociable and will share nests with other adults. Individuals communicate with loud "churring" sounds. Courtship and mating happen almost as soon as the adults awaken in spring, and rearing the young is a race against time. If the summer is not a productive one—with trees failing to provide enough of the right kind of food—the breeding effort might be abandoned; there is no point in raising litters that cannot fatten up enough to survive the next winter.

Life is difficult enough for the edible dormouse without the threat of persecution by people. But the animal can be such a nuisance that in much of Europe it has been trapped or poisoned to the brink of extinction. Ironically, one of the few places it seems to be doing well is in England, where it is an introduced species and therefore not entitled to any protection.

burrow or tree stump the animals can sleep undisturbed for several months. Cool, damp, relatively constant conditions in the soil allow maximum efficiency in hibernation, ensuring the animal's fat reserves last as long as possible.

Glis are superb climbers owing largely to the flexible pads on the soles of their feet. The pads secrete a sticky substance that enhances grip and allows the dormouse to scamper up completely smooth, vertical surfaces. Glimpsed briefly, edible dormice can be mistaken for small squirrels, but closer inspection reveals the

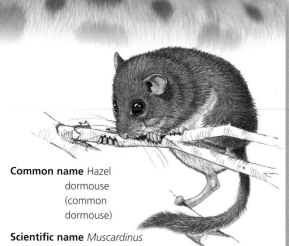

Common name Hazel dormouse (common dormouse)

Scientific name *Muscardinus avellanarius*

Family Gliridae

Order Rodentia

Size Length head/body: 2.5–3.5 in (6–9 cm); tail length: 2–3 in (5.5–7.5 cm)

Weight 0.5–1.4 oz (14–40 g)

Key features Small dormouse with bright-yellow fur and long, furry tail; face short; eyes large and black; ears small but prominent

Habits Nocturnal; social; arboreal; hibernates 6 months of the year

Breeding One or 2 litters of 2–7 (usually 3–5) young born in midsummer after gestation period of 22–24 days. Weaned at 40 days; sexually mature at about 11 months. May live up to 6 years in captivity, at least 5 in the wild

Voice Generally silent, but may utter small, chirping contact sounds; wheezes when disturbed asleep

Diet Nuts, seeds, flowers and buds, fruit, and insects; occasionally eggs and baby birds

Habitat Deciduous woodland with dense understory of nut-bearing trees such as hazel; also mature hedgerows

Distribution Western and central mainland Europe, except northern Scandinavia, Iberian Peninsula, and Turkey

Status Population: probably about 2 million; IUCN Lower Risk: near threatened

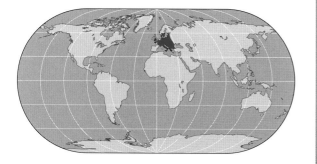

Hazel Dormouse

Muscardinus avellanarius

Known the world over as the drowsiest guest at the Mad Hatter's tea party in Lewis Carroll's Alice in Wonderland, *the common dormouse is becoming rare in parts of its native European range.*

IN MANY WAYS THE HAZEL dormouse seems like an animal from another era. It was well known a century ago, when woodland management was an important part of the rural economy. Large areas of woodland were managed by a traditional technique called coppicing. It involved cutting trees down to a stump from which numerous new trunks would sprout. Trees managed by coppicing stay young and vigorous indefinitely. Coppiced hazel trees were especially useful to humans because their trunks grow into straight poles. They also make exceptionally good dormouse habitat, with rapid new growth and crops of nuts every fall, not to mention crevices among the trunks where the dormice could wedge their winter hibernation nests. Often when the woodcutters were at work, they would disturb dormice; but since only small areas were coppiced at a time, there was always a refuge nearby.

Preference for Hazel Trees

Hazel is particularly important for this species and is usually prominent in its habitat. It provides caterpillars in spring and nuts in the fall. Other important plants for dormice include honeysuckle, strips of which are used to weave tight nests. Bramble is important, too, offering dense cover and food, with flowers in the summer and sweet fruits later in the year.

Hazel dormice are completely at home in the trees and find all their food among the branches. Their feet have long toes and thick pads to provide grip. The long, furry tail serves as a counterbalance, allowing the animal to scamper along the narrowest branches. Dormice

SEE ALSO Dormouse, Edible **7**:104

leap from branch to branch with complete confidence, even in the dark. They are sociable animals, and summer nests are usually built in clusters. The nests of breeding females are almost twice as large as those of solitary animals, about 5 inches (12 cm) in diameter. They are made up of a woven ball of grass and soft, shredded bark or honeysuckle. Young families from different mothers may be put into one nest to form a nursery. Juvenile dormice often remain together after their mother has abandoned them at about 40 days of age.

Deep Sleepers

Hibernation in dormice is extremely deep. Before hibernating, each dormouse boosts its energy reserves and fattens up as much as possible. But even for a well-prepared animal, the winter energy budget is extremely tight. Once asleep, the body temperature drops steadily with the outside temperature. It will fall to within a quarter of a degree of zero, just

warm enough to prevent its blood from freezing. The heartbeat and breathing rate fall too—it can be difficult to tell if a hibernating dormouse is alive or dead. However, when it senses an increase in the outside temperature, the dormouse comes slowly wheezing and quivering back to life. It may have lost over a third of its body weight over winter.

Common dormice have declined across much of their native range thanks largely to habitat loss and changes in woodland management. Many large woodlands that once supported dormice have been fragmented by networks of roads and other developments, leaving patches too small to support viable populations. Dormice need more space than other small rodents, and isolated populations stand little chance of being boosted by immigration, since dormice do not travel far. One solution, tried successfully in England, is to reintroduce captive-bred dormice to forests where they once lived. Yet that only works if traditional woodland management methods are restored, and the dormice are provided with nest boxes and food to help them settle in.

⊕ Two hazel dormice eating a chestnut. Nuts are a favored food for the species, which finds all its food within the branches of trees.

The Gundi Family

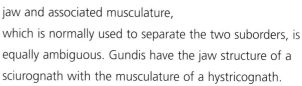

A small family of desert-dwelling rodents, gundis have been known to science for a little over 220 years. The five species of gundi are small, squat rodents with legs so short that the belly brushes along the ground as they walk. There is a short tail, which in *Ctenodactylus* species is wispy and brushlike, like a sawn-off version of a tree squirrel's tail. In the other three species it is more substantial.

There are four digits on each foot, each with a small, sharp claw. On the hind feet the inner two toes also bear comblike rows of stiff bristles. They are used for grooming the gundi's fur. Such unusual structures give the group its family name, Ctenodactylidae, which translates literally as "comb fingers." Careful grooming is necessary in maintaining the gundi's fur. It is dense, long, soft, and warm, providing vital insulation in the chill desert night.

Gundis have huge eyes and rounded ears. All gundis have acute hearing, but the round earflaps of the central Saharan or mzab gundi are completely joined to the sides of its head so it cannot move them at all. The ear holes are furry to prevent them filling with windblown sand. Gundi teeth are arranged in the typical rodent pattern, but the incisors lack the front coating of hard enamel that makes most rodents such efficient gnawing animals.

Origins and Questions

The ctenodactylids are a very ancient group, with the earliest recognizable fossils appearing about 45 million years ago in mid-Eocene rock deposits in Asia. In later times there were gundis in southern Europe, Asia, and Africa. The living genera are all quite recent, having evolved from a common ancestor in North Africa, probably some time in the last million or so years. The gundis appeared about the same time as the sciurognath and hystricognath evolutionary lines diverged, and there is still considerable debate over which group the gundis really belong to. Outwardly gundis look something like a cross between a squirrel and a guinea pig or cavy. The structure of the jaw and associated musculature, which is normally used to separate the two suborders, is equally ambiguous. Gundis have the jaw structure of a sciurognath with the musculature of a hystricognath.

Lifestyle

Gundis live in small groups, sheltering in narrow rock crevices and never in burrows. In loose sandy soils their homes would be prone to collapse and easily unearthed by predators. Gundis are able to squeeze into extremely tight spaces thanks to a highly flexible rib cage. Gundi "dens" are spartan and often drafty, with no nesting material. The animals rely on their thick fur, shared body heat, and the warmth retained by the rocks to provide some respite from the cold at night. Individual gundis are not territorial, and neither are they aggressive. They forage alone, but sleep together at night. They communicate using birdlike calls. Sharp chirps or foot drumming usually signal an alarm.

Gundis are diurnal. Their huge eyes are designed for seeing in the gloom of their dens rather than in the darkness of night. The animals are generally active early

---

Family: Ctenodactylidae, 4 genera, 5 species

Ctenodactylus 2 species, desert gundi (*C. vali*); North African gundi (*C. gundi*)

Felovia 1 species, felou gundi (*F. vae*)

Massoutiera 1 species, mzab gundi (*M. mzabi*)

Pectinator 1 species, Speke's gundi (*P. spekei*)

⊖ The mzab or Lataste's gundi inhabits rocky outcrops in the desert and mountain regions of North and West Africa. It is distinctive among gundis for its immovable earflaps.

born in a highly advanced state, fully furred and alert, with their eyes open. Despite being so well developed, they remain in the breeding den for several weeks. Right from the start they are left alone by the mother while she goes out foraging. They call to her constantly for food and milk, using a continuous chirruping noise.

Where Gundis Live

All five gundi species live in desert and semidesert regions of North Africa. However, apart from the desert gundis (*Ctenodactylus*) that occupy overlapping ranges in Morocco, Algeria, Tunisia, and Libya, the ranges of the remaining four genera hardly overlap at all. The felou gundi is found only in the western Sahara states of Mali and Mauritania, and possibly Senegal. The mzab gundi occurs only in the central Sahara in parts of southern Algeria, Niger, and Chad. Speke's gundi is restricted to Ethiopia, Somalia, and northern Kenya.

and late in the day, and shelter from the worst of the sun's heat around midday. Their diet is vegetarian. Leaves and stems are nibbled and plucked from plants, since gundi incisors are not suited to gnawing, unlike those of most rodents.

Their continuously growing molars, however, are more than up to the task of grinding leaves and stems of desert plants. The more succulent the food, the better, since gundis do not drink and must get all the water they need from what they eat. Food can be difficult to find, and gundis often have to wander a long way (many hundreds of meters) from their den when foraging.

Gundis breed just once a year and have a long gestation for such small animals. Young are

⊙ Three gundi species with their own distinctive vocalizations: Speke's gundi (1) has a rich vocabulary of sounds; the felou gundi (2) makes a harsh "chee-chee" call if in trouble; the mzab gundi (3) is relatively silent.

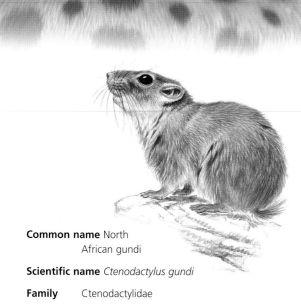

Common name North African gundi

Scientific name *Ctenodactylus gundi*

Family Ctenodactylidae

Order Rodentia

Size Length head/body: 6–8 in (16–21 cm); tail length: 0.5–1 in (1–2.5 cm)

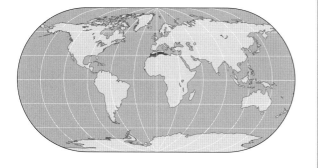

Weight Up to 10 oz (300 g)

Key features Low-slung body with short legs and large head; fur thick, soft, and pale buffy-brown, sometimes pinkish; eyes large; ears round, furry, and flattened against head; inner 2 toes on back feet have comblike bristles

Habits Diurnal; shelters in rock crevices; does not burrow; social and nonterritorial; active all year round; does not store food or hibernate

Breeding Single litter of 1–3 well-developed young born in spring after gestation period of 55 days. Weaned at 4 weeks; sexually mature at 9–12 months. May live up to 5 years in captivity, probably fewer in the wild

Voice Quiet, birdlike chirping calls; also drums feet when agitated

Diet Desert plants

Habitat Semidesert and desert

Distribution North Africa from Morocco to Libya

Status Population: unknown, but relatively abundant locally

North African Gundi

Ctenodactylus gundi

The charming North African gundi, with its large eyes and powder-puff fur, is much tougher than it looks. It manages to make a living in a harsh, arid landscape where food, water, and other creature comforts are always in short supply.

A TYPICAL DAY IN THE LIFE of a North African gundi starts early, as soon as the sun is up. Nights are cold, so the first activity of the day is a spot of sunbathing. Like all mammals, the gundi is capable of regulating its body temperature by metabolizing food, but it is more economical to let the sun's energy help do the job as well.

Conserving Water

Once the temperature is comfortably warm, the gundi sets off to forage. It is still early, and there will be dew on the leaves and plant stems. That moisture and the juices of plants are the only water the gundi ever takes on board. After feeding, the gundi lies in the sun again, and the heat it absorbs helps speed up the digestion process. Four or five hours after sunrise the desert becomes uncomfortably hot. The gundi cannot afford to sweat the precious water it

has taken into its body to keep cool, so it retreats to the shadowy depths of a deep rock crevice for a rest. It will emerge for another bout of feeding later if need be, but the rest of its waking hours are spent socializing with other members of the group.

Gundi colonies usually consist of half a dozen or so individuals, sometimes as many as 11. There are one or two adult males and a few females and their young. Relationships within the group seem amicable, and the animals regularly indulge in play. Individuals

⊕ A North African gundi in Tunisia absorbs the heat of the early morning sun before foraging. When the sun gets too hot, gundis seek the shade of a rock crevice in which to rest.

communicate using chirping calls to warn each other of danger. In the silence of the desert predators such as birds and snakes have evolved to hunt almost noiselessly, and gundis, along with many other desert rodents, have acute hearing. At any sign of danger the animals disappear into the nearest available hiding place. Their collapsible rib cage and flat ears allow them to squeeze into what seem like impossibly tight spaces. Despite their short legs, gundis move at an impressive speed and can climb up almost vertical rock faces.

Young gundis are born in an advanced state after a long pregnancy. They can see and run quickly right away, and they have fur at birth. They need the covering for warmth, since there is no warm bedding in the den. They are capable of eating leaves almost immediately. The vegetation is brought by their mother, who chews it before feeding it to her family. However, the babies are not fully weaned for four weeks. Their mother's milk serves as a supplement to their diet rather than a staple, because she cannot spare much water from her own body.

Desert Relative

The North African gundi shares the southern part of its range with its close relative the desert gundi. The two species look alike but sound quite different—the desert gundi whistles rather than chirps. As a result, members can recognize their own species.

Gundis are still relatively little known; but with their large eyes, gentle temperament, soft fur, and sweet birdlike calls, they are appealing creatures. It has been suggested that they might one day become popular pets.

111

List of Genera

The following lists all the genera of rodents in the suborder Sciurognathi:

Order Rodentia (Part)

SUBORDER SCIUROGNATHI

FAMILY APLODONTIDAE

Aplodontia Mountain beaver (sewellel)

FAMILY SCIURIDAE
Squirrels, chipmunks, marmots, and prairie dogs

SUBFAMILY SCIURINAE
Ammospermophilus Antelope squirrels
Atlantoxerus Barbary ground squirrel
Callosciurus Oriental tree squirrels
Cynomys Prairie dogs
Dremomys Red-cheeked squirrels
Epixerus African palm squirrels
Exilisciurus Pygmy squirrels
Funambulus Asiatic palm squirrels
Funisciurus Rope squirrels
Glyphotes Sculptor squirrel
Heliosciurus Sun squirrels
Hyosciurus Sulawesi long-nosed squirrels
Lariscus Striped ground squirrels
Marmota Marmots
Menetes Indochinese ground squirrel
Microsciurus Dwarf squirrels
Myosciurus African pygmy squirrel
Nannosciurus Black-eared squirrel
Paraxerus Bush squirrels
Prosciurillus Sulawesi dwarf squirrels
Protoxerus African giant squirrels
Ratufa Oriental giant squirrels
Rheithrosciurus Tufted ground squirrel
Rhinosciurus Shrew-faced squirrel
Rubrisciurus Sulawesi giant squirrel
Sciurillus Neotropical pygmy squirrel
Sciurotamias Asian rock squirrels
Sciurus Tree squirrels
Spermophilopsis Long-clawed ground squirrel
Spermophilus Ground squirrels
Sundasciurus Sunda squirrels
Syntheosciurus Bangs' mountain squirrel
Tamias Chipmunks
Tamiasciurus Red squirrels
Tamiops Asiatic Striped squirrels
Xerus African ground squirrels

SUBFAMILY PETAURISTINAE
Aeretes North Chinese flying squirrel
Aeromys Large black flying squirrels
Belomys Hairy-footed flying squirrel
Biswamoyopterus Namdapha flying squirrel
Eupetaurus Woolly flying squirrel
Glaucomys New World flying squirrels
Hylopetes Arrow-tailed flying squirrels
Iomys Horsfield's flying squirrels
Petaurillus Pygmy flying squirrels
Petaurista Giant flying squirrels
Petinomys Dwarf flying squirrels
Pteromys Eurasian flying squirrels
Pteromyscus Smoky flying squirrel
Trogopterus Complex-toothed flying squirrel

FAMILY CASTORIDAE Beavers

Castor Beavers

FAMILY GEOMYIDAE Pocket gophers

Geomys Eastern pocket gophers
Orthogeomys Giant pocket gophers
Pappogeomys Mexican pocket gophers
Thomomys Western pocket gophers
Zygogeomys Michoacan pocket gopher (tuza)

FAMILY HETEROMYIDAE
Pocket mice, kangaroo rats, and kangaroo mice

SUBFAMILY DIPODOMYINAE
Dipodomys Kangaroo rats
Microdipodops Kangaroo mice

SUBFAMILY HETEROMYINAE
Heteromys Forest spiny pocket mice
Liomys Spiny pocket mice

SUBFAMILY PEROGNATHINAE
Chaetodipus/Perognathus Coarse-haired or silky pocket mice

FAMILY DIPODIDAE Jerboas

SUBFAMILY ALLACTAGINAE
Allactaga Four- and five-toed jerboas
Allactodipus Bobrinski's jerboa
Pygeretmus Fat-tailed jerboas

SUBFAMILY CARDIOCRANIINAE
Cardiocranius Five-toed pygmy jerboa
Salpingotus Three-toed pygmy jerboas

SUBFAMILY DIPODINAE
Dipus Northern three-toed jerboa
Eremodipus Lichtenstein's jerboa
Jaculus Desert jerboas
Stylodipus Three-toed jerboas

SUBFAMILY EUCHOREUTINAE
Euchoreutes Long-eared jerboa

SUBFAMILY PARADIPODINAE
Paradipus Comb-toed jerboa

SUBFAMILY SICISTINAE
Sicista Birch mice

SUBFAMILY ZAPODINAE
Eozapus Chinese jumping mouse
Napaeozapus Woodland jumping mouse
Zapus Jumping mice

FAMILY MURIDAE
Rats, mice, voles, lemmings, hamsters, and gerbils

SUBFAMILY ARVICOLINAE
Alticola Mountain voles
Arborimus Tree voles
Arvicola Water voles
Blanfordimys Afghan voles
Chionomys Snow voles
Clethrionomys Red-backed voles
Dicrostonyx Collared lemmings
Dinaromys Martino's snow vole
Ellobius Mole voles
Eolagurus Yellow steppe lemmings
Eothenomys South Asian voles
Hyperacrius Kashmir voles
Lagurus Steppe lemming
Lasiopodomys Brandt's voles
Lemmiscus Sagebrush vole
Lemmus Brown lemmings
Microtus Meadow voles
Myopus Wood lemming
Neofiber Round-tailed muskrat
Ondatra Muskrat
Phaulomys Japanese voles
Phenacomys Heather voles
Proedromys Duke of Bedford's vole
Prometheomys Long-clawed mole vole
Synaptomys Bog lemmings
Volemys Musser's voles

SUBFAMILY CALOMYSCINAE
Calomyscus Mouselike hamsters

SUBFAMILY CRICETINAE
Allocricetulus Mongolian hamsters
Cansumys Gansu hamster
Cricetulus Dwarf hamsters
Cricetus Black-bellied hamster
Mesocricetus Golden hamsters
Phodopus Small desert hamsters

Tscherskia Greater long-tailed hamster

SUBFAMILY CRICETOMYINAE
Beamys Long-tailed pouched rats
Cricetomys African giant pouched rats
Saccostomus Pouched mice

SUBFAMILY DENDROMURINAE
Dendromus African climbing mice
Dendroprionomys Velvet climbing mouse
Deomys Congo forest mouse (link rat)
Leimacomys Groove-toothed forest mouse
Malacothrix Gerbil mouse (large-eared mouse)
Megadendromus Nikolaus's mouse
Prionomys Dollman's tree mouse
Steatomys Fat mice

SUBFAMILY GERBILLINAE
Ammodillus Ammodile
Brachiones Przewalski's gerbil
Desmodilliscus Pouched gerbil
Desmodillus Cape short-eared gerbil
Gerbillurus Hairy-footed gerbils
Gerbillus Gerbils
Meriones Jirds
Microdillus Somali pygmy gerbil
Pachyuromys Fat-tailed gerbil
Psammomys Sand rats
Rhombomys Great gerbil
Sekeetamys Bushy-tailed jird
Tatera Large Naked-soled gerbils
Taterillus Small naked-soled gerbils

SUBFAMILY LOPHIOMYINAE
Lophiomys Crested rat (maned rat)

SUBFAMILY MURINAE
Abditomys Luzon broad-toothed rat
Acomys African spiny mice
Aethomys African rock rats
Anisomys Squirrel-toothed or powerful-toothed rat
Anonymomys Mindoro rat
Apodemus Field mice
Apomys Philippine forest mice
Archboldomys Mount Isarog shrew mouse
Arvicanthis African or unstriped grass rats
Bandicota Bandicoot rats
Batomys Hairy-tailed rats
Berylmys White-toothed rats
Bullimus Philippine rats
Bunomys Hill rats
Carpomys Luzon tree rats
Celaenomys Blazed luzon shrew rat
Chiromyscus Fea's tree rat
Chiropodomys Pencil-tailed tree mice
Chiruromys Tree mice
Chrotomys Philippine striped rats
Coccymys Brush mice
Colomys African water rat
Conilurus Rabbit rats
Coryphomys Buhler's rat
Crateromys Bushy-tailed cloud-rats
Cremnomys Indian rats
Crossomys Earless water rat
Crunomys Philippines shrew rats
Dacnomys Millard's rat
Dasymys Shaggy African marsh rats
Dephomys Defua rats
Desmomys Harrington's rat
Diomys Crump's or Manipur mouse
Diplothrix Ryukyu rat
Echiothrix Sulawesi spiny rat
Eropeplus Sulawesi soft-furred rat
Golunda Indian bush rat
Grammomys African thicket rats
Hadromys Manipur bush rat
Haeromys Ranne mice
Hapalomys Marmoset rats
Heimyscus African smoky mouse
Hybomys Striped mice
Hydromys Water rats
Hylomyscus African wood mice
Hyomys New Guinean giant rats
Kadarsanomys Sody's tree rat

Komodomys Komodo rat
Lamottemys Mount Oku rat
Leggadina Australian native mice
Lemniscomys Striped grass mice
Lenomys Trefoil-toothed giant rat
Lenothrix Gray tree rat
Leopoldamys Long-tailed giant rats
Leporillus Australian stick-nest rats
Leptomys New Guinean water rats
Limnomys Mindanao mountain rat
Lophuromys Brush-furred rats
Lorentzimys New Guinea jumping mouse
Macruromys New Guinea rats
Malacomys African swamp rats
Mallomys Woolly rats
Margaretamys Margareta's rats
Mastomys Multimammate mice
Maxomys Oriental spiny rats
Mayermys One-toothed shrew mouse
Melasmothrix Sulawesian shrew-rat
Melomys Mosaic-tailed rats
Mesembriomys Tree rats
Microhydromys Lesser shrew mice
Micromys Eurasian harvest mouse
Millardia Asian soft-furred rats
Muriculus Striped-backed mouse
Mus Old World mice
Mylomys African groove-toothed rat
Myomys African mice
Neohydromys Mottled-tailed shrew mouse
Nesokia Short-tailed bandicoot rats
Niviventer White-bellied rats
Notomys Australian hopping mice
Oenomys Rufous-nosed rats
Otomys African vlei rats
Palawanomys Palawan soft-furred
   mountain rat
Papagomys Flores Island giant tree rats
Parahydromys Coarse-haired water rat
Paraleptomys Montane water rats
Parotomys Whistling rats
Paruromys Sulawesian giant rats
Paulamys Flores long-nosed rat
Pelomys Groove-toothed swamp rats
Phloeomys Giant cloud rats
Pithecheir Sunda tree rats
Pogonomelomys New Guinean brush mice
Pogonomys Prehensile-tailed tree mice
Praomys African soft-furred mice
Pseudohydromys New Guinea shrew mice
Pseudomys Australian mice
Rattus Old World rats
Rhabdomys Four-striped grass
Rhynchomys Shrew rats
Solomys Naked-tailed rats
Spelaeomys Flores cave rat
Srilankamys Ohiya rat
Stenocephalemys Ethiopian narrow-headed
   rats
Stenomys Slender rats
Stochomys Target rat
Sundamys Giant Sunda rats
Taeromys Sulawesi rats
Tarsomys Long-footed rats
Tateomys Greater Sulawesian shrew rats
Thallomys Acacia rats
Thamnomys Thicket rats
Tokudaia Ryukyu spiny rats
Tryphomys Luzon short-nosed rat
Uranomys Rudd's mouse
Uromys Giant naked-tailed rats
Vandeleuria Long-tailed climbing mice
Vernaya Red climbing mouse
Xenuromys Rock-dwelling giant rat
Xeromys False water rat
Zelotomys Broad-headed mice
Zyzomys Australian rock rats

SUBFAMILY MYOSPALACINAE
Myospalax Zokors

SUBFAMILY MYSTROMYINAE
Mystromys White-tailed mouse

SUBFAMILY NESOMYINAE
Brachytarsomys White-tailed rat
Brachyuromys Short-tailed rats
Eliurus Tufted-tailed rats
Gymnuromys Voalavoanala
Hypogeomys Malagasy giant rat or votsotsa
Macrotarsomys Big-footed mice
Nesomys Island mouse

SUBFAMILY PETROMYSCINAE
Delanymys Delany's swamp mouse
Petromyscus Rock mice

SUBFAMILY PLATACANTHOMYINAE
Platacanthomys Malabar spiny dormouse
Typhlomys Chinese pygmy dormouse

SUBFAMILY RHIZOMYINAE
Cannomys Lesser bamboo rat
Rhizomys Bamboo rats
Tachyoryctes Root rats or African mole rats

SUBFAMILY SIGMODONTINAE
Abrawayaomys Ruschi's rat
Aepeomys Montane mice
Akodon Grass mice
Andalgalomys Chaco mice
Andinomys Andean mouse
Anotomys Ecuador fish-eating rat
Auliscomys Big-eared mice
Baiomys American pygmy mice
Bibimys Crimson-nosed rats
Blarinomys Brazilian shrew-mouse
Bolomys Bolo mice
Calomys Vesper mice
Chelemys Greater long-clawed mice
Chibchanomys Chibchan water mouse
Chilomys Colombian forest mouse
Chinchillula Altiplano chinchilla mouse
Chroeomys Altiplano mice
Delomys Atlantic forest rats
Eligmodontia Gerbil mice
Euneomys Chinchilla mice
Galenomys Garlepp's mouse
Geoxus Long-clawed mole mouse
Graomys Leaf-eared mice
Habromys Crested-tailed deer mice
Hodomys Allen's woodrat
Holochilus Marsh rats
Ichthyomys Crab-eating rats
Irenomys Chilean climbing mouse
Isthmomys Isthmus rats
Juscelinomys Juscelin's mice
Kunsia South American giant rats
Lenoxus Andean rat
Megadontomys Giant deer mice
Melanomys Dusky rice rats
Microryzomys Small rice rats
Neacomys Bristly mice
Nectomys Neotropical water rats
Nelsonia Diminutive wood rats
Neotoma Wood rats
Neotomodon Mexican volcano mouse
Neotomys Andean swamp rat
Nesoryzomys Galápagos mice
Neusticomys Fish-eating rats
Notiomys Edwards' long-clawed mouse
Nyctomys Vesper rat
Ochrotomys Golden mouse
Oecomys Arboreal rice rats
Oligoryzomys Pygmy rice rats
Onychomys Grasshopper mice
Oryzomys Rice rats
Osgoodomys Michoacan deer mouse
Otonyctomys Hatt's vesper rat
Ototylomys Big-eared climbing rat
Oxymycterus Hocicudos
Peromyscus Deer mice
Phaenomys Rio de Janeiro arboreal rat
Phyllotis Leaf-eared mice
Podomys Florida mouse
Podoxymys Roraima mouse
Pseudoryzomys Brazilian false rice rat
(ratos-do-mato)
Punomys Puna mouse

Reithrodon Bunny rat
Reithrodontomys American harvest mice
Rhagomys Brazilian arboreal mouse
Rheomys Central American water mice
Rhipidomys American climbing mice
Scapteromys Swamp rat
Scolomys Spiny mice
Scotinomys Brown mice
Sigmodon Cotton rats
Sigmodontomys Rice water rats
Thalpomys Cerrado mice
Thomasomys Thomas' oldfield mice
Tylomys Naked-tailed climbing rats
Wiedomys Red-nosed mouse
Wilfredomys Wilfred's mice
Xenomys Magdalena rat
Zygodontomys Cane mice

SUBFAMILY SPALACINAE
Nannospalax Lesser blind mole rats
Spalax Greater blind mole rats

FAMILY ANOMALURIDAE
Scaly-tailed squirrels

SUBFAMILY ANOMALURINAE
Anomalurus Scaly-tailed flying squirrels

SUBFAMILY ZENKERELLINAE
Idiurus Pygmy scaly-tailed flying squirrels
Zenkerella Cameroon scaly-tailed squirrel

FAMILY PEDETIDAE

Pedetes Springhare (springhaas)

FAMILY CTENODACTYLIDAE Gundis

Ctenodactylus Common gundis
Felovia Felou gundi
Massoutiera Mzab gundi
Pectinator Pectinator or East African gundi

FAMILY MYOXIDAE Dormice

SUBFAMILY GRAPHIURINAE
Graphiurus African dormice

SUBFAMILY LEITHIINAE
Dryomys Forest dormice
Eliomys Garden dormice
Myomimus Mouse-tailed dormice
Selvinia Desert dormouse

FAMILY MYOXINAE

Glirulus Japanese dormouse
Muscardinus Hazel dormouse
Myoxus Edible or fat dormouse

Glossary

Words in SMALL CAPITALS refer to other entries in the glossary.

Adaptation features of an animal that adjust it to its environment; may be produced by evolution—e.g., camouflage coloration

Adaptive radiation when a group of closely related animals (e.g., members of a FAMILY) have evolved differences from each other so that they can survive in different NICHES

Adult a fully grown animal that has reached breeding age

Anal gland (anal sac) a gland opening by a short duct either just inside the anus or on either side of it

Aquatic living in water

Arboreal living among the branches of trees

Arid zones dry, desert areas with low annual rainfall

Arthropod animals with a jointed outer skeleton, e.g., crabs and insects

Biodiversity a variety of SPECIES and the variation within them

Biped any animal that walks on two legs. See QUADRUPED

Breeding season the entire cycle of reproductive activity from courtship, pair formation (and often establishment of TERRITORY), through nesting to independence of young

Browsing feeding on leaves of trees and shrubs

Cache a hidden supply of food; also (verb) to hide food for future use

Canine (tooth) a sharp stabbing tooth usually longer than rest

Canopy continuous (closed) or broken (open) layer in forests produced by the intermingling of branches of trees

Capillaries tiny blood vessels that convey blood through organs from arteries to veins

Carnivore meat-eating animal

Carrion dead animal matter used as a food source by scavengers

Cecum blind sac in the digestive tract opening out from the junction between the small and large intestines. In herbivorous mammals it is often very large; it is the site of bacterial action on CELLULOSE. The end of the cecum is the appendix; in SPECIES with a reduced cecum the appendix may retain an antibacterial function

Cellulose the material that forms the cell walls of plants

Cementum hard material that coats the roots of mammalian teeth. In some SPECIES, cementum is laid down in annual layers that, under a microscope, can be counted to estimate the age of individuals

Cheek pouch a pouch used for the temporary storage of food, found only in the typical monkeys of the OLD WORLD

Cheek teeth teeth lying behind the CANINES in mammals, consisting of PREMOLARS and MOLARS

CITES Convention on International Trade in Endangered Species. An agreement between nations that restricts international trade to permitted levels through a system of licensing and administrative controls. Rare animals and plants are assigned to categories: (for instance Appendix 1, 2). See Volume 1 page 17

Congenital condition animal is born with

Coniferous forest evergreen forests found in northern regions and mountainous areas dominated by pines, spruces, and cedars

Corm underground food storage bulb of certain plants

Crepuscular active in twilight

Deciduous forest dominated by trees that lose their leaves in winter (or the dry season)

Deforestation the process of cutting down and removing trees for timber or to create open space for activities such as growing crops

Delayed implantation when the development of a fertilized egg is suspended for a variable period before it implants into the wall of the UTERUS and completes normal pregnancy. Births are thus delayed until a favorable time of year

Den a shelter, natural or constructed, used for sleeping, giving birth, and raising young; also (verb) the act of retiring to a den to give birth and raise young or for winter shelter

Dental formula a convention for summarizing the dental arrangement, in which the numbers of all types of tooth in each half of the upper and lower jaw are given. The numbers are always presented in the order: INCISOR (I), CANINE (C), PREMOLAR (P), MOLAR (M). The final figure is the total number of teeth to be found in the skull. A typical example for Carnivora would be I3/3, C1/1, P4/4, M3/3 = 44

Dentition an animal's set of teeth

Desert area of low rainfall dominated by specially adapted plants such as cacti

Diastema a space between the teeth, usually the INCISORS and CHEEK TEETH. It is typical of rodents and lagomorphs, although also found in UNGULATES

Digit a finger or toe

Digitigrade method of walking on the toes without the heel touching the ground. See PLANTIGRADE

Dispersal the scattering of young animals going to live away from where they were born and brought up

Display any relatively conspicuous pattern of behavior that conveys specific information to others, usually to members of the same SPECIES; can involve visual or vocal elements, as in threat, courtship, or greeting displays

Diurnal active during the day

DNA (deoxyribonucleic acid) the substance that makes up main part of the chromosomes of all living things; contains genetic code that is handed down from generation to generation

Domestication process of taming and breeding animals to provide help and useful products for humans

Dormancy a state in which—as a result of hormone action—growth is suspended and metabolic activity reduced to a minimum

Dorsal relating to the back or spinal part of the body; usually the upper surface

Droppings see FECES and SCATS

Ecosystem a whole system in which plants, animals, and their environment interact

Edentate toothless, but is also used as group name for anteaters, sloths, and armadillos

Endemic found only in one geographical area, nowhere else

Estivation inactivity or greatly decreased activity in hot or dry weather

Estrus the period when eggs are released from the female's ovaries, and she becomes available for successful mating. Estrous females are often referred to as "in heat" or "RECEPTIVE" to males

Eurasian distributed across all or part of both Europe and Asia

Eutherian mammals that give birth to babies, not eggs, and rear them without using a pouch on the mother's belly

Extinction process of dying out in which every last individual dies, and the SPECIES is lost forever

Family technical term for a group of closely related SPECIES that often also look quite similar. Zoological family names always end in "idae." See Volume 1 page 11. Also used as the word for a social group within a species consisting of parents and their offspring

Feces remains of digested food expelled from the body as pellets. Often accompanied by SCENT secretions

Feral domestic animals that have gone wild and live independently of people

Flystrike where CARRION-feeding flies have laid their eggs on an animal

Fossorial adapted for digging and living in burrows or underground tunnels

Frugivore an animl that eats fruit as main part of the diet

Fur mass of hairs forming a continuous coat characteristic of mammals

Fused joined together

Gape wide-open mouth

Gene the basic unit of heredity enabling one generation to pass on characteristics to its offspring

Generalist an animal that is capable of a wide range of activities, not specialized

Genus a group of closely related SPECIES. The plural is genera. See Volume 1 page 11

Gestation the period of pregnancy between fertilization of the egg and birth of the baby

Grazing feeding on grass

Gregarious living together in loose groups or herds

Guard hairs long, shiny hairs that project from UNDERFUR, particularly prominent in some AQUATIC RODENTS and CARNIVORES

Harem a group of females living in the same TERRITORY and consorting with a single male

Herbivore an animal that eats plants (grazers and browsers are thus herbivores)

Heterodont DENTITION specialized into CANINES, INCISORS, and PREMOLARS, each type of tooth

having a different function. See HOMODONT

Hibernation becoming inactive in winter, with lowered body temperature to save energy. Hibernation takes place in a special nest or DEN called a hibernaculum

Homeothermy maintenance of a high and constant body temperature by means of internal processes

Home range the area that an animal uses in the course of its normal periods of activity. See TERRITORY

Homodont DENTITION in which the teeth are all similar in appearance and function

Hybrid offspring of two closely related SPECIES that can interbreed, but the hybrid is sterile and cannot produce offspring of its own

Inbreeding breeding among closely related animals (e.g., cousins) leading to weakened genetic composition and reduced survival rates

Incisor (teeth) simple pointed teeth at the front of the jaws used for nipping and snipping

Indigenous living naturally in a region; NATIVE (i.e., not an introduced SPECIES)

Insectivore animals that feed on insects and similar small prey. Also used as a group name for animals such as hedgehogs, shrews, and moles

Interbreeding breeding between animals of different SPECIES or varieties within a single FAMILY or strain; can cause dilution of the gene pool

Interspecific between SPECIES

Intraspecific between individuals of the same SPECIES

IUCN International Union for the Conservation of Nature, responsible for assigning animals and plants to internationally agreed categories of rarity. See table below

Juvenile young animal that has not yet reached breeding age

Keratin tough, fibrous material that forms hairs, feathers, and protective plates on the skin of VERTEBRATE animals

Lactation process of producing milk in MAMMARY GLANDS for offspring

Larynx voice box where sounds are created

Latrine place where FECES are left regularly, often with SCENT added

Leptospirosis disease caused by leptospiral bacteria in kidneys and transmitted via urine

Mammary glands characteristic of mammals, glands for production of milk

Matriarch senior female member of a social group

Metabolic rate rate at which chemical activities occur within animals, including the exchange of gasses in respiration and the liberation of energy from food

Metabolism the chemical activities within animals that turn food into energy

Migration movement from one place to another and back again, usually seasonal

Molars large crushing teeth at the back of the mouth

Molt process in which mammals shed hair, usually seasonal

Monogamous animals that have only one mate at a time

Montane in a mountain environment

Musk mammalian SCENT

Mutation random changes in genetic material

Native belonging to that area or country, not introduced by human assistance

Natural selection when animals and plants are challenged by natural processes (including predation and bad weather) to ensure survival of the fittest

New World the Americas; OLD WORLD refers to the non-American continents (not usually Australia)

Niche part of a habitat occupied by an ORGANISM, defined in terms of all aspects of its lifestyle

Nocturnal active at night

Nomadic animals that have no fixed home, but wander continuously

Old World non-American continents. See NEW WORLD

Olfaction sense of smell

Omnivore an animal that eats almost anything, meat or vegetable

Opportunistic taking advantage of every varied opportunity that arises; flexible behavior

Opposable fingers or toes that can be brought to bear against others on the same hand or foot in order to grip objects

IUCN CATEGORIES

EX **Extinct**, when there is no reasonable doubt that the last individual of a species has died.

EW **Extinct in the Wild**, when a species is known only to survive in captivity or as a naturalized population well outside the past range.

CR **Critically Endangered**, when a species is facing an extremely high risk of extinction in the wild in the immediate future.

EN **Endangered**, when a species faces a very high risk of extinction in the wild in the near future.

VU **Vulnerable**, when a species faces a high risk of extinction in the wild in the medium-term future.

LR **Lower Risk**, when a species has been evaluated and does not satisfy the criteria for CR, EN, or VU.

DD **Data Deficient**, when there is not enough information about a species to assess the risk of extinction.

NE **Not Evaluated**, species that have not been assessed by the IUCN criteria.

Order a subdivision of a class of animals consisting of a series of related animal FAMILIES. See Volume 1 page 11

Organism any member of the animal or plant kingdom; a body that has life

Ovulation release of egg from the female's ovary prior to its fertilization

Pair bond behavior that keeps a male and a female together beyond the time it takes to mate; marriage is a "pair bond"

Parasite an animal or plant that lives on or within the body of another

Parturition process of giving birth

Pelage furry coat of a mammal

Pheromone SCENT produced by animals to enable others to find and recognize them

Physiology the processes and workings within plants and animal bodies, e.g., digestion. Maintaining a warm-blooded state is a part of mammal physiology

Placenta the structure that links an embryo to its mother during pregnancy, allowing exchange of chemicals between them

Plantigrade walking on the soles of the feet with the heels touching the ground. See DIGITIGRADE

Polygamous when animals have more than one mate in a single mating season. MONOGAMOUS animals have only a single mate

Polygynous when a male mates with several females in one BREEDING SEASON

Population a distinct group of animals of the same SPECIES or all the animals of that species

Population dynamics changes in abundance and age structure of a population

Posterior the hind end or behind another structure

Predator an animal that kills live prey for food

Prehensile grasping tail or fingers

Premolars teeth found in front of the MOLARS, but behind the CANINES

Primate a group of mammals that includes monkeys, apes, and ourselves

Promiscuous mating often with many mates, not just one

Protein chemicals made up of amino acids. Essential in the diet of animals

Quadruped an animal that walks on all fours (a BIPED walks on two legs)

Range the total geographical area over which a SPECIES is distributed

Receptive when a female is ready to mate (in ESTRUS)

Reproduction the process of breeding, creating new offspring for the next generation

Retina light-sensitive layer at the back of the eye

Retractile capable of being withdrawn, as in the claws of typical cats, which can be folded back into the paws to protect them from damage when walking

Riparian living beside rivers and lakes

Roadkill animals killed by road traffic

Rodent animals belonging to the most numerous order of mammals, the Rodentia. All have a characteristic dentition, with a pair of large, continually growing incisor teeth that are often visible even when the mouth is closed

Ruminant animals that eat vegetation and later bring it back from the stomach to chew again ("chewing the cud" or "rumination") to assist its digestion by microbes in the stomach

Savanna tropical grasslands with scattered trees and low rainfall, usually in warm areas

Scats fecal pellets, especially of CARNIVORES. SCENT is often deposited with the pellets as territorial markers

Scent chemicals produced by animals to leave smell messages for others to find and interpret

Scrotum bag of skin within which the male testicles are located

Scrub vegetation dominated by shrubs—woody plants usually with more than one stem

Secondary forest trees that have been planted or grown up on cleared ground

Siblings brothers and sisters

Social behavior interactions between individuals within the same SPECIES, e.g., courtship

Species a group of animals that look similar and can breed to produce fertile offspring

Steppe open grassland in parts of the world where the climate is too harsh for trees to grow

Sub-Saharan all parts of Africa lying south of the Sahara Desert

Subspecies a locally distinct group of animals that differ slightly from normal appearance of SPECIES; often called a race

Symbiosis when two or more SPECIES live together for their mutual benefit more successfully than either could live on its own

Syndactylous fingers or toes that are joined along their length into a single structure

Taxonomy the branch of biology concerned with classifying ORGANISMS into groups according to similarities in their structure, origins, or behavior. The categories, in order of increasing broadness, are: SPECIES, GENUS, FAMILY, ORDER, class, and phylum. See Volume 1 page 11

Terrestrial living on land

Territory defended space

Thermoregulation the maintenance of a relatively constant body temperature either by adjustments to METABOLISM or by moving between sunshine and shade

Torpor deep sleep accompanied by lowered body temperature and reduced METABOLIC RATE

Translocation transferring members of a SPECIES from one location to another

Tundra open grassy or shrub-covered lands of the far north

Ultrasounds sounds that are too high-pitched for humans to hear

Underfur fine hairs forming a dense, woolly mass close to the skin and underneath the outer coat of stiff hairs in mammals

Ungulate hoofed animals such as pigs, deer, cattle, and horses; mostly HERBIVORES

Uterus womb in which embryos of mammals develop

Ventral belly or underneath of an animal (opposite of DORSAL)

Vertebrate animal with a backbone (e.g., fish, mammals, reptiles), usually with a skeleton made of bones, but sometimes softer cartilage

Vibrissae sensory whiskers, usually on snout, but can be on areas such as elbows, tail, or eyebrows

Viviparous animals that give birth to active young rather than laying eggs

Vocalization making of sounds such as barking and croaking

Zoologist person who studies animals

Zoology the study of animals

Further Reading

General

Cranbrook, G., **The Mammals of Southeast Asia**, Oxford University Press, New York, NY, 1991

Eisenberg, J. F., and Redford, K. H., **The Mammals of the Neotropics**, University of Chicago Press, Chicago, IL, 1999

Estes, R. D., **The Behavioral Guide to African Mammals**, University of California Press, Berkley, CA, 1991

Garbutt, N., **The Mammals of Madagascar**, Pica Press, Sussex, U.K., 1999

Harrison, D. L., and Bates, P. P. J. J., **The Mammals of Arabia**, Sevenoaks, U.K., 1991

Kingdon, J., **The Kingdon Field Guide to African Mammals**, Academic Press, San Diego, CA, 1997

MacDonald, D., **Collins Field Guide to the Mammals of Britain and Europe**, Harper Collins, New York, NY, 1993

MacDonald, D., **The Encyclopedia of Mammals**, Barnes and Noble, New York, NY, 2001

Nowak, R. M., **Walker's Mammals of the World**, The John Hopkins University Press, Baltimore, MD, 1999

Skinner, J. D., and Smithers, R. H. N., **The Mammals of the Southern African Subregion**, University of Pretoria, Pretoria, South Africa, 1990

Strahan, R., **The Mammals of Australia**, Reed New Holland, Australia, 1998

Whitaker, J. O., **National Audubon Society Field Guide to North American Mammals**, Alfred A. Knopf, New York, NY, 1996

Wilson, D. E., **The Smithsonian Book of North American Mammals**, Smithsonian Institution Press, Washington, DC, 1999

Wilson, D. E., and Reeder, D. M., **Mammal Species of the World. A Taxonomic and Geographic Guide,** Smithsonian Institution Press, Washington, DC, 1999

Young, J. Z., **The Life of Mammals: Their Anatomy and Physiology**, Oxford University Press, Oxford, U.K., 1975

Specific to this volume

Alderton, D., **Rodents of the World**, Blandford, London, U.K., 1999

Craves, R. A., **The Prairie Dog: Sentinel of the Plains**, Texas Technical University Press, Austin, TX, 2001

Hannney, P. W., **Rodents**, David and Charles, Newton Abbot, U.K., 1975

Hart, M., **Rats**, Allison and Busby/Schocken Books, New York, NY, 1982

Lacy, E. A., Patton, J. L., and Cameron G. N., **Life Underground: The Biology of Subterranean Rodents**, Chicago University Press, Chicago, NY, 2000

Steele, M., and Koprowski, J. L., **North American Tree squirrels**, Smithsonian Institution Press, Washington, DC, 2001

Wells-Gosling, N., **Flying Squirrels**, Smithsonian Institution Press, Washington, DC, 1985

Useful Websites

General

http://animaldiversity.ummz.umich.edu/
University of Michigan Museum of Zoology animal diversity websites. Search for pictures and information about animals by class, family, and common name. Includes glossary

http://www.cites.org/
IUCN and CITES listings. Search for animals by scientific name, order, family, genus, species, or common name. Location by country and explanation of reasons for listings

http://endangered.fws.gov
Information about threatened animals and plants from the U.S. Fish and Wildlife Service, the organization in charge of 94 million acres (38 million ha) of American wildlife refuges

http://www.iucn.org
Details of species and their status; listings by the International Union for the Conservation of Nature, also lists IUCN publications

http://www.nccnsw.org.au
Website for threatened Australian species

http://www.ewt.org.za
Website for threatened South African wildlife

http://www.panda.org
World Wide Fund for Nature (WWF), newsroom, press releases, government reports, campaigns

http://www.aza.org
American Zoo and Aquarium Association

http://www.ultimateungulate.com
Guide to world's hoofed mammals

http://www.wcs.org
Website of the Wildlife Conservation Society

http://www.nwf.org
Website of the National Wildlife Federation

http://www.nmnh.si.edu/msw/
Mammals list on Smithsonian Museum site

http://www.press.jhu.edu/books/walkers_mammals_of_the_world/prep.html
Text of basic book listing species, illustrating almost every genus

Specific to this volume

spot.colorado.edu/~halloran/sqrl.html
Tree squirrels in North America

http://www.rmca.org/
Rat and Mouse Club of America. Includes club information, events, contests, merchandise, and rat standards

http://www.ratworld.com/
Information and forums for rat lovers: rats, rodents, mice, pets

http://www.glirarium.de/dormouse/
General website for information on dormice

netvet.wustl.edu/rodents.htm
Compilation of resources on rodents, mostly from veterinary viewpoint

http://www.webcom.com/lstead/rodents/rodents.html
Basic information on pet rodents

http://www.alienexplorer.com/ecology/topic24.html
Squirrels and chipmunks

http://www.squirrels.org/
General squirrel information

http://www.ngpc.state.ne.us/wildlife/flysqu.html
Habits, reproduction, and management of flying squirrels

http://www.deadsquirrel.com
Squirrels as pests, fun too!

members.tripod.com/srl2/
Squirrel Rights League, thinks squirrels have been given a bad name

Set Index

A **bold** number shows the volume and is followed by the relevant page numbers (e.g., **1:** 52, 74).

Common names in **bold** (e.g., **aardwolf**) mean that the animal has an illustrated main entry in the set. Underlined page numbers (e.g., **9:** 78–79) refer to the main entry for that animal.

Italic page numbers (e.g., **2:** 103) point to illustrations of animals in parts of the set other than the main entry.

Page numbers in parentheses—e.g., **1:** (24)—locate information in At-a-Glance boxes.

Animals that get main entries in the set are indexed under their common names, alternative common names, and scientific names.

Picture Credits

Abbreviations

FLPA	Frank Lane Picture Agency
NHPA	Natural History Photographic Agency
NPL	naturepl.com
OSF	Oxford Scientific Films

t = top; b = bottom; c = center; l = left; r = right

Jacket

tl caracal, Pete Oxford/naturepl.com; tr group of dolphins, Robert Harding Picture Library; bl lowland gorilla, Martin Rügner/Naturphotographie; br Rothchild's giraffe, Gerard Lacz/FLPA

8–9 John Brown/OSF; **10** Anthony Bannister/NHPA; **13** Ken Preston-Mafham/Premaphotos Wildllife; **14–15** Robin Redfern/Ecoscene; **16** K. Maslowski/FLPA; **18–19** Mary Ann McDonald/NPL; **20–21** Minden Pictures/FLPA; **22–23** François Gohier/Ardea; **24–25** Wendy Shattil & Bob Rozinski/OSF; **26–27** Jeff Foott/NPL; **28–29** François Gohier/Ardea; **29** Tom & Pat Leeson; **30–31** Alan & Sandy Carey/OSF; **32–33** Janos Jurka/Bruce Coleman Collection; **33** Mark Hamblin/OSF; **34–35** Pete Oxford/NPL; **36–37** Clem Haagner/Ardea; **37** Joe McDonald/Corbis; **38–39** S. Roberts/Ardea; **39** Raymond Gehman/Corbis; **40** OSF; **40–41** Liz & Tony Bomford/Ardea; **42–43** Rob Jordan/Bruce Coleman Collection; **44** Copyright © Frederick Warne & Co., 1903, 2002 Reproduced by permission of Frederick Warne & Co.; **44–45** Manfred Danegger/NHPA; **46–47** Jeff Foott/NPL; **48–49** Niall Benvie/OSF; **50–51** Lynn Stone/NPL; **52–53** W. Wisniewski/OSF; **54-55** Daniel J. Cox/OSF; **56–57** Rod Planck/NHPA; **58–59** Wendy Shattil & Bob Rozinski/OSF; **59** Mark Hamblin/OSF; **60–61** Steve Maslowski/FLPA; **62–63** Ken Preston-Mafham/Premaphotos Wildlife; **65** Kathie Atkinson/OSF; **67** Jean-Paul Ferrero/Ardea; **68–69**, **70** Rodger Jackman/OSF; **70–71** Adrian Davies/NPL; **72–73** Andy Purcell/ICCE; **74** Bettmann/Corbis; **74–75** Stephen Dalton/NHPA; **75** James L. Amos/Corbis; **76–77** Andy Purcell/ICCE; **78–79** Robin Redfern/OSF; **80–81** B. Moose Peterson/Ardea; **82–83** S. & D. & K. Maslowski/FLPA; **84–85** Åke Lindau/Ardea; **86–87** Dennis Avon/Ardea; **88–89** Andrey Zvoznikov/Ardea; **90–91** Paal Hermansen/NHPA; **92–93** R. Wilmshurst/FLPA; **94–95**, **96–97** Tom Ulrich/OSF; **98–99** Tony Tilford/OSF; **100–101** Eyal Bartov/OSF; **102–103** Michel Strobing/Survival Anglia/OSF; **104–105** Alastair MacEwen/OSF; **106–107** Silvestris Fotoservice/FLPA; **108–109** W. George; **110–111** Thorsten Stegmann

Artists

Denys Ovenden, Priscilla Barrett with Michael Long, Graham Allen, Malcolm McGregor

While every effort has been made to trace the copyright holders of illustrations reproduced in this book, the publishers will be pleased to rectify any omissions or inaccuracies.

For Reference

Not to be taken

from this library